MW00906289

The Truth
About
The Truth

This book belongs to:

Vicki Salato

DEDICATION

This book is dedicated to everyone who has experienced their own crisis of faith

FOREWORD

Jehovah's Witnesses claim to be a Christian based denomination which is well known worldwide for their door-to-door evangelism. They believe that Jehovah is the only true God, Jesus Christ is God's Son as well as the archangel Michael, and that the Holy Spirit is nothing more than the power of God. Boasting more than 7 million members around the globe (in 2009), they profess a high standard of morality, a strict sense of unity, and claim to be the only ones preaching real biblical truth to the masses.

Who *are* these people?

This book answers that question in detail from the perspective of a former member of the Jehovah's Witnesses who was born and raised into the denomination. This book provides a first-person point of view on what it was like to live the lifestyle, abide by the doctrines, and the emotional hardships involved in awakening to, and leaving, the sect.

This book was written for those who are studying with Jehovah's Witnesses, leaving the Jehovah's Witnesses, relatives to a Jehovah's Witness, or who simply know a Jehovah's Witness.

*Since this book is based upon the Jehovah's Witness culture, all scripture quotes in this book are from the New World Translation of the Holy Scriptures, unless otherwise noted.

A WORD FROM THE AUTHOR

This book details my personal experience as a second-generation Jehovah's Witness. Although my parents did not become Jehovah's Witnesses until after they married, it was the only life that I ever knew growing up, as they had been Witnesses for several years by the time I came along. As with any child who is born and raised into a denomination, I didn't question the adults who taught me because I believed that the adults knew what they were talking about. By the time I had grown enough to do my *own* thinking the doctrine had become so ingrained that I took it for granted and accepted it as truth.

Being that I wasn't familiar with anything else, I didn't think it was strange to shun the holidays, ignore birthdays, and refrain from school sports programs. I thought nothing unusual about spending a week every summer at large Jehovah's Witness conventions, or spending my Saturday mornings trying to win converts from house to house. I was taught that the Bible version we used was superior to any other Bible version, and so I tested all ideals and doctrines against my Bible version's passages. Although I wasn't a perfect member of the faith (and who was?), I was very devout and believed everything they taught me whether I understood it or not. I was "In the Truth" and had no inclination to change my mind on the matter.

And then came the year 2004.

It was early January, and I was 35 years old; God began to show me things that, for lack of a better phrase, *totally* blew my mind! He ripped the blinders off my eyes, causing me to see my religion for what it really was – it was intriguing yet frightening! From that point forward, my life was permanently changed as I started seeking *real* truth, and *real* Christianity through Christ instead of through an organization. By the end of November that same year, at the age of 36, I cut my ties with the denomination permanently.

Since the Jehovah's Witnesses continually seek to add converts to their numbers, I decided I should write this book so potential converts can know *exactly* what they're getting themselves into. However, I must state that in light of their constant spiritual "progression", some things have changed since I left, therefore a new convert's experience may be somewhat different than mine. For example, they have made some changes in the printing of their Watchtower and Awake magazines, in the congregational leadership, and in their meeting schedules, among other things. In spite of these changes, though, the facts regarding Watchtower history, its doctrine, and its flawed practices remain the same.

I'm not trying to preach to anyone, and I'm not trying to be disparaging to the Jehovah's Witnesses. My purpose is to provide a candid look into the life of a Jehovah's Witness and their belief system, and let you, the reader, judge the matter for yourself.

Yours in Christ,

Tami Dickerson

* *Most names throughout this book have been changed to ensure individuals' privacy.*

Table of Contents

Chapter 1
Introduction To My World

I was born the eighth of nine siblings – six boys and three girls. We grew up in a respectable, middle class neighborhood on the South Side of Elmira, New York. Ours was a pretty decent neighborhood with a mix of elderly widows, middle-aged couples, and young families. With plenty of kids in the neighborhood, and having so many siblings of my own, there was always someone to do something with. We did most of the usual things kids do: Played in each others yards, made "exclusive" clubs, built forts, and got into the occasional argument. Our next door neighbors, Lena and Rob, had a granddaughter, Sherry, who visited them overnights so often that she was pretty much a part of the neighborhood too. But even when Sherry wasn't around, Lena and Rob still liked to have us neighborhood kids come visit with them on their front porch.

We spent our Winters building snow forts, Springs enjoying the lilacs, Summers sleeping out in the yard with a tent, and Autumns jumping in leaf piles. We had our share of hot cocoa and home made bread, family vacations, and back yard barbecues. I remember many a lazy summer's day splashing in a pool, and many a winter's day romping in the snow.

But of course, it wasn't *always* idyllic: We had all of us and only *one* bathroom. We had our sibling fights. We had our school problems. We resisted chores. We got too loud. We came home too late sometimes. We *all* gave our share of grey hairs to Dad and Mom!

In spite of the normal issues that come with a large family we were generally happy and healthy growing up. We didn't have to deal with alcoholism, drug addiction, domestic violence, guns, or gang issues. Our public playground down the street was well kept and boasted a free public pool with plenty of supervision. Even our schools were in walking distance, so we didn't have to put up with school bus shenanigans either.

Yes, we were very blessed to be raised in such a good neighborhood.

Money was tight with a family as big as ours, but Dad and Mom were resourceful: For many years Dad cultivated a vegetable garden and we always helped with the upkeep and harvesting of the vegetables; we had a large yard, therefore we had a large garden filled with at least a dozen kinds of vegetables. Dad also knew how to keep the family car going, which saved loads of money on mechanic's bills. My older brother, Gil, also had a talent for tinkering with the car, and together he and Dad could keep a car going forever, or so it seemed. As for Mom, she had a talent for canning the garden produce which she stored away in our pantry. She didn't stop there though, as she also learned to make home-made pickles and home made yogurts, and used a food dehydrator for long term storage. She also had a hand cranked food grinder that was used for making home made baby food.

Her abilities extended beyond the kitchen; she was also a very talented seamstress and made most of our clothing. She was equally talented with crocheting, knitting, embroidery and needlepoint. Mom often received compliments on her abilities, and many people thought that her creations were actually store-bought items.

Beyond gardens, home car repair, and tailoring our clothes, they also found other ways to save money. I remember when Mom worked as a Weight Watchers counselor in Owego NY, about forty-five minutes away from home. Owego had a "Dollar Night" at the movies every Monday – Yup, a dollar for each person to watch the latest movie! Every so often Dad would take us to Owego to watch a movie while Mom was at work. After the movie we'd go play at a local park until Mom was done working – I'll always remember those times!

Although we didn't have a lot of money for recreational things, we always found something fun and interesting to do. We lived within walking distance of some forested hills (South Mountain, Chamberlain's Hill, and Mount Zoar Hill) and we often went hiking the trails and exploring. If it weren't the hills, we'd go exploring down at Seeley Creek, which ran along the foot of the hills. Sometimes we'd find a fossil rock with worm holes; sometimes we'd find crawdads, sometimes we'd just hike through the trails next to the creek. Other times we'd stay close to home and take a small pail to hunt for, and collect, weird bugs (yeah, even us girls would do that!). We'd fill the pail with dirt, topped with a few pebbles and maybe some foliage, and start turning over stones to search for bugs. I always liked the millipedes, but the pill bugs were pretty cool too. Sometimes we'd find something and had no clue what it was! One time my sister, Amelia, and I found a caterpillar. We put it in a large glass jar with some grass and a long stick. The next day, we looked and saw that it made a chrysalis! Unfortunately, we weren't careful enough, and the chrysalis met an unfortunate end. We felt terrible about it.

I'll never forget the time my brother, Quentin, found a nest of black spiders hiding out behind our trash containers (they weren't black widows). He took a large glass jar and put several of them in it. About an hour later Dad was complaining to him about the creepy jar....when Quentin went to get it, all the spiders were crumpled up, dead, at the bottom – he didn't realize they'd all kill each other!

We also used to go around collecting cool looking stones and pebbles in our pails. We'd find some with colored layers, some with colored flecks, some with odd shapes, etc. and compare what we found. Quentin once found a large, silvery rock someplace and brought it home. We all thought it was really cool and broke it up into pieces so everyone could have some of it. We didn't find out until *years* later that it was graphite.

And, of course, we almost always had a swimming pool in the back yard. It was only three feet deep, but it was enough for cooling off in the summer! Quite often the neighborhood kids would come over and we'd all be playing and splashing, and making up water games. I remember one time, me and Amelia went to go splash around, but we saw a butterfly already in the water. It was upside-down, stuck to the water on it's wings with its legs frantically flailing. We gently took it out and set it on a rock. Once it's wings dried, it flew away. We were quite happy with ourselves for helping the poor creature – especially since we had the chrysalis fiasco still in the backs of our minds!

And off course, we had to drain the pool every so often because we'd get bored with the pool and leave it alone for a while....and some time later when we went to jump in again, it would be *filled* with hatched mosquito larvae swimming around. Ugh! "Dad, we need to dump the pool again!"

With such a large brood to raise, Mom made sure we learned to pull our own weight around the house. When any of us reached the age of nine or ten she'd start teaching us how to cook. She'd start us off by having us help her with a recipe, teaching us how to measure and mix and things like that. Gradually we'd get to where each of us could do an entire recipe ourselves. By our late teens, we were taking turns planning the family menu for the week, with her oversight, of course; and we took turns cooking entire suppers for the family.

She and Dad both taught us how to sort and wash laundry, and each of us had an assigned laundry day each week. To teach us about budgeting, we were paid our allowances according to the chores we did throughout the week: Each chore paid out its own particular amount. Not only was that an incentive to do the chores, but it taught us to earn our pay – no free hand outs! We also learned to earn extra money in the neighborhood as well: My older brothers would mow lawns for the elderly who lived nearby, and us younger ones would rake lawns in the autumn and shovel sidewalks in the winter to earn our extra money. By the time any of us was old enough to seek real employment we had a solid work ethic and a foundation for the budgeting skills we needed.

Beyond giving us love, life skills, and providing for our physical needs, our parents also tried their best to provide for our spiritual needs. Since we were Jehovah's Witnesses, this took up a lot of time during the week because Jehovah's Witnesses spend a lot of time studying their own doctrine.

Although neither Dad nor Mom were were raised into the Jehovah's Witness faith they were brought into it by a woman named Mabel; an older woman who came knocking on their door several years after they married. My sister, Laurel, and brother, Chad, were the only two siblings that ever had a Christmas, a Thanksgiving, or Birthday party because they were born before my parents became Witnesses.

The following pages document my own personal experience growing up as a Jehovah's Witness.

Chapter 2
Overview of the Jehovah's Witness Life

The Jehovah's Witnesses are a progressive religious group who live a very moral, and extremely conservative, lifestyle. As of September 2009, Jehovah's Witnesses numbered over 7 million worldwide in over 230 lands, with branch offices peppered throughout, enabling the entire brotherhood to receive the same information and materials at the same time. Jehovah's Witnesses consider themselves to be true Christians who seek complete unity in their ranks and strive for complete submission to God (Jehovah) and His visible Organization on earth. They also seek to remain separate from the world and desire to *not* blend in with mainstream Christianity. Jehovah's Witnesses are led by the Governing Body, a group of men headquartered in Brooklyn, New York. This headquarters is also referred to as "Brooklyn", "Bethel", (which means "House of God"), "The Watchtower Bible and Tract Society", "The Faithful and Discreet Slave", and "The Organization". All Jehovah's Witness rules, regulations, doctrine, Bible study assignments and literature originate in the headquarters. Jehovah's Witnesses believe that The Organization is God's sole channel of communication for mankind, therefore they live by everything that The Organization instructs (*The Watchtower, October 1, 1994, p. 8*) To be a Jehovah's Witness meant being "In The Truth".

The core doctrine of Jehovah's Witnesses goes something like this :

> *Jesus Christ returned invisibly in 1914, the year that was the beginning of the "End Times". At this time, Jesus inspected the religions on the Earth to see who was the "Faithful and Discreet Slave" properly feeding Jehovah's people real spiritual food; Jesus found that the leadership of The Bible Students (who later were renamed Jehovah's Witness) were the only*

ones faithfully doing so. This meant that the group had Jehovah's blessing and would be the sole channel of true spiritual food for mankind. When the time is right, God will cause a world-wide Armageddon that will destroy "this system of things", including wickedness, evil, and those who have rejected The Truth as published through the "Faithful and Discreet Slave". At this time Satan the Devil will be imprisoned in the spiritual abyss, and there will be a thousand years of peace under Christ's rulership, known as The New Order. During this thousand year reign there will be 144,000 chosen people, a.k.a "the anointed ones", a.k.a. "The Little Flock", who will be in heaven to rule with Christ. Jehovah has been choosing these anointed ones ever since the beginning of the Christian congregation in Bible times. Everyone else who remains and yet isn't part of the 144,000 are considered to be non-anointed, and will stay on the Paradise Earth. These ones staying on Earth are called "the Great Crowd". During this time of paradise, all truth loving people who have died will be resurrected to live in the New Order paradise to live forever. The New Testament was written primarily for the anointed ones and therefore can only be truly understood by these anointed ones. The anointed are the only ones in the New Covenant with Jesus, therefore they are the only ones who get to take the Wine and Unleavened Bread during the yearly communion service ("The Memorial"). Jesus is the mediator only for the anointed, though the Great Crowd are saved by their association with the anointed ones. Only Jehovah's Witnesses have The Truth, all other Christian denominations are feeding at the tables of demons (Christendom is look upon with utter disdain).

This is why Jehovah's Witnesses must go door-to-door preaching their doctrine; it is an act of charity and love to preach to the masses who are duped by the satanic lies that run rampant through Christendom. To become a Jehovah's Witness, and then leave the faith later, makes one an enemy of Jehovah.

This means that, in their eyes, I am now an enemy of Jehovah.

Growing up as a Jehovah's Witness meant going to the Bible meetings at the Kingdom Hall three times each week. The Kingdom Hall is the meeting house for Jehovah's Witnesses and is purposely meant to look as little like a church as possible: No steeples, no stained glass windows, and rows of individual seats instead of pews. Instead of a collection plate being passed around they have "contribution boxes" set aside, and anyone can contribute whatever money they wanted at any time, as there was no formal collection time. There was no Sunday School for adults or children as everyone was expected to meet together in the main auditorium to hear the same information at the same time, regardless of age, in the name of unity. They do not refer to their meeting house as a "church", preferring the title "Kingdom Hall" instead. They do not have any regularly scheduled fellowship groups.

Forming special prayer groups, fellowship groups, or study groups outside of Bethel's direction was completely discouraged, with claims of concern that people may misinterpret scripture and be confused in The Truth. According to their publication *"Our Kingdom Ministry"*, the September 2007 issue in the Question Box section (paragraphs 1-2), they state that the "faithful and discreet slave" does not approve of any Bible study group or Bible literature that is not under its direct oversight.

Jehovah's Witnesses also have their own version of a hymnal, which is not referred to as a hymnal but is instead referred to as a "Song Book". These songs are doctrinally specific to Jehovah's Witness teaching; you won't find "Amazing Grace" or "Be Thou My Vision" in these hymnals. Jehovah's Witnesses also have their own unique Bible version, *"The New World Translation of the Holy Scriptures"*, which is also printed specific to their beliefs. Although it reads nearly like any other modernized Bible version, there are some differences that reflect their doctrine. This can readily be seen in passages such as John 1:1 (*"...the word was with God and the word was a god"*) and throughout the New Testament where they replace the word "Lord" with *"Jehovah"* on a frequent basis.

The Jehovah's Witnesses also claim that they do not have a clergy-laity system, but it has been my experience that this claim is untrue. Instead of Pastors or Priests, the Jehovah's Witnesses have Elders who lead the congregation, and Ministerial Servants who serve in a deacon's role. Elders and Ministerial Servants are to be a baptized male, unless there isn't enough baptized males in the congregation to fill the vacancy. In such a case, a baptized female will be chosen, though she would relinquish her position as soon as a qualified baptized male became available. During my time of membership, there was also an Elder assigned in each congregation to oversee the others, and his title would be "The Presiding Overseer". Elders lead the congregation within the confines of The Organization's direction and are responsible for: Baptisms, leading worship, weddings, Bible meetings, evangelism, congregational events, home visitations, funerals, and biblical counseling. Only the Elders can perform the Elders' tasks, and none of the regular members were to perform any of the Ministerial Servants' tasks. There was a definite rank and order to this. Jehovah's Witness Elders and Ministerial Servants however, are not financially supported by the congregation and are expected to earn their own living. Many of them are self-employed. Beyond the Elders and the Ministerial Servants, everyone else was just a regular member of the congregation. To have one's husband become an Elder was an honor, and to have one's son become a Ministerial Servant was a secondary honor.

Yes, there is a definite clergy-laity system in the Jehovah's Witness faith. Of course, they deny this, stating that all baptized members are considered to be ordained ministers, but this claim rings hollow in light of the fact that only the Elders can serve as congregational leaders and perform the tasks normally expected by a church Pastor.

The congregation I grew up in had more than 150 members altogether, therefore we had several Elders and Ministerial Servants. As time went on, the membership outgrew the Kingdom Hall building so that the congregation was split into two and shared the Hall (one group met in the morning, the other met in the afternoon). It isn't uncommon for a congregation to split and share; in fact, such occurrences were always viewed as a sign of Jehovah's blessing on the congregations.

Congregations within a geographical area are grouped together into "circuits" and were overseen by a special Elder called a "Circuit Overseer". Circuit Overseers would travel from congregation to congregation on a continual basis, spending a week at a time with each one. In most cases they would make arrangements to stay at a member's home during the week he visited, though I'd heard that some Kingdom Halls had special apartments built into them especially for the Circuit Overseer. His basic job was to provide assistance with each congregation's individual needs, make sure the congregations were operating according to The Organization's instructions, and provide encouragement for the door-to-door proselytizing program that the Jehovah's Witnesses are known for. An Elder served as a Circuit Overseer for a specified amount of time before being replaced by another.

The Circuit Overseer's visit was always a special week: Everyone made a special effort to attend all the meetings for the week, and made an even bigger effort to go out in the door-to-door ministry. Some members would make arrangements to invite the Circuit Overseer and his wife to their homes for supper. Sometimes, after a Circuit Overseer's visit was finished, the members of the congregation would be asked to donate money to the family who hosted him in order to defray the expense of boarding him for that week.

As for the weekly worship meetings, they were always scripted and conducted exactly as prescribed by The Organization:

On a typical Sunday, the congregation gathers at the Kingdom Hall to listen to the "Public Talk" for the first part of the meeting (basically, a sermon). Quite often the Public Talk is orated by an Elder in the congregation, though frequently we also had "guest speakers" from other congregations within the circuit who gave the Talk (these guest speakers are also Elders). The second half of the Sunday meeting is spent reading and answering questions from an assigned article of indoctrination from the denomination's *"The Watchtower"* Magazine. The basic format is this: An Elder would be chosen to be the Study Conductor for that week, and he would stand at the podium. Near him would be seated a baptized male member who was chosen as that week's "Reader". The Study conductor would introduce the article to be studied, and cue the Reader when to read a paragraph. The Reader usually reads only one paragraph at a time, while in between paragraphs the Conductor would ask a prepared question or two that was pre-written by The Organization for each paragraph. The members of the congregation participate in answering by raising their hands and being called on by the Conductor. Another designated brother in the congregation would run a microphone over to the member chosen to answer. That was how the whole Watchtower Study would progress until the article was finished. Occasionally, a guest speaker for the public talk would be running late for arrival for some reason or another, in which case we'd have the Watchtower Study *first*, and then listen to the Public Talk afterward.

These Sunday meetings usually lasted about two hours, with a small break for singing between the Public Talk and the Watchtower Study. When I was a member, the Public Talk lasted for about 45 minutes, though nowadays they have been pared down to only 30 minutes long. About once or twice per year we'd have a special guest come and give a slide show on a doctrinal topic, a missionary experience, or something else specific to the Jehovah's Witness faith. We'd have the slide show in lieu of the Public Talk. These were always a treat, especially as a child.

The second meeting of the week was on Tuesday evenings, when we had the "Book Study". Small groups would gather at the Kingdom Hall and in members' homes to study material from assigned books published by the Watchtower, Bible and Tract Society. These meetings usually lasted about one hour, and were similar to the Watchtower Study format: A study conductor would cue the reader, and the members would answer pre-written questions paragraph by paragraph.

These small book study groups were always arranged by the Elders: Each family was assigned to meet with a certain group; whether it be the Kingdom Hall group or a group in a member's home. This was done to avoid overcrowding in members' homes. Periodically, for various reasons, the Elders would re-arrange the book study assignments and we would start attending at a different member's home. Many of these small groups would host a "Goody Night" each month. These were nights in which the members of that particular study group would bring a dish-to-pass, and after the meeting was finished we'd all share in the yummy delights. Attendance was *always* full on Goody Night.

When I was very young, we used to meet for our book study at Hazel Cheney's home. She was a lovely, elderly woman, and we called her "Grandma Cheney". She had the kind of home that just made you feel comfortable the minute you walked in! Soft cushy armchairs, Victorian wallpaper, antique shaded lamps; very "home-y"! After the study session was finished, all of us children in the study group would gather at the large chalk board that Grandma Cheney had on her entry wall and entertain ourselves while the adults fellowshipped.

Years later, in the 1990's, my parents gained the privilege of hosting a study at their own home each week. For Goody Night, mom would always prepare a hearty dish, such as Italian stuffed shells or chili with meat. She figured that since so many people would bring sugary and dessert-y items, she'd provide something more supper-like for those who didn't have a chance to eat before the meeting. Mom was always thoughtful like that.

On Thursday evenings we had the Theocratic Ministry School and Service Meetings, back to back. These were basically meetings designed to hone the members' skills in Bible reading and evangelizing. Although it was called a "school", these were ongoing programs that never actually ended. These meetings consisted of Bible readings, skits depicting situations in which to evangelize, and review of the *"Our Kingdom Ministry"* sheet. The Kingdom Ministry sheets were basically a few pages of articles, questions associated with the articles, and a few bits of Jehovah's Witness announcements and information. These meetings ended past nine o'clock at night, meaning many of the very young children would fall asleep on their parents' laps during these meetings.

Not only was it important to attend all of these meetings, but it was equally important to be "prepared" for each meeting. Preparation meant studying the material ahead of time so you could have comments ready for the question and answer sessions, which translated into a LOT of studying throughout the week. The announcements in the Kingdom Ministry sheet always told us which materials to study for the upcoming Tuesday and Thursday meetings, and the Watchtower magazines always had the month's study outline listed inside it's front cover, so we always knew exactly what to be studying and when. Because the Jehovah's Witness culture is centered around complete unity within the membership, we knew that all the congregations would be studying the exact same thing during their meeting times. This made it nice on the occasions we'd decide to visit other congregations within our circuit, as our prepared lessons would be the same as theirs.

As a Jehovah's Witness, you were expected to dress nicely for each meeting, including the small in-home study groups: The females were all expected to wear dresses or skirts, and the males were all expected to wear dress shirts and ties. Of course, all clothing was expected to be modest: No cleavage showing, hemlines should end below the knees, men's hair shouldn't be long enough to touch the collar, etc.

Because there was so much studying involved in the meetings, we spent a lot of time during the week preparing for these meetings. On Saturdays we'd all gather in the living room while Dad conducted the family Watchtower study in preparation for the Sunday meeting. We'd each take turns reading a paragraph and answering the corresponding questions. Dad would also have us read all the unquoted Bible references that were peppered throughout the paragraphs. *And* we had to finish the Watchtower study, even if it took us all afternoon! We were just kids, and the studies were just plain boring. Between reading and discussing all the unquoted scriptures, and trying to wrap our minds around some of the complicated explanations of doctrine in the articles, it sometimes took two hours to get through the stuff. And that was just on Saturday *afternoons*! In the *mornings* on Saturdays, Mom would conduct a family study with us for an hour from other Watchtower Society literature that *wasn't* assigned for meetings. Mom would faithfully study with us for an hour every Saturday morning; I remember Mom going through such books as " *The Great Teacher*", "*Paradise Lost*", and "*Your Youth*". But Saturdays didn't stop with just those two studies. Two Saturdays each month, we'd join in with the door-to-door evangelizing. Yep. So, between the morning family study, the afternoon Watchtower study, and the Saturdays that we also did the evangelizing, our Saturdays didn't leave a lot of time off for play.

Monday nights we had another family study in preparation for the Tuesday night book study group. It was basically another tedious family gathering in the living room, taking turns reading and answering the corresponding pre-written questions from a book assigned by The Organization. And, again, we would plod through the study because many of us younger ones didn't understand things, and we had to read all the scriptures, and it could take a lot of time.

Wednesday nights were a little better. Basically we gathered around and simply took turns reading through the assigned Bible passages for the Thursday night meeting – no questions involved. Since children didn't generally receive Kingdom Ministry sheets, we didn't have to study those; that was for the adults only. However, once you were old enough to read well enough, you were encouraged sign up for the Theocratic Ministry School skits and talks. I signed up when I was eight years old. Being a member of the Ministry School meant that, on a few occasions throughout the year, it would be your turn to present a little scenario depicting an evangelizing situation to the congregation if you were female, or present a brief oration on a Bible topic or passage if you were male. To join the Theocratic Ministry School was a mark of your growing spirituality.

On top of the regularly scheduled meetings and the study prep times during the week, we also had the *"Daily Text"* and the *"Year Book"* readings each night at the supper table, through the suggestion of The Organization. The Daily Text was basically a daily scripture devotional for each day of the year published by the Watchtower Society, and each year a new edition would come out. After we were done eating supper, Dad would bring out the devotional and read it, after which we'd discuss the scripture as a family. After that, Mom would bring out the latest edition of the Jehovah's Witness Year Book and read several pages from it. (The *Year Book* basically relayed experiences from Jehovah's Witness pioneers and missionaries from around the world). We would all sit, dutifully, around the supper table listening to the readings.

Then, of course, there were the more "recreational" methods of indoctrination that were available: The Watchtower Society also published audio tapes, video tapes, and CD ROMs of Jehovah's Witness hymnal music, Bible readings, and dramas. My parents ensured that we always had the latest release of media material. If we weren't studying for a meeting, we were reading devotionals, and if we weren't doing that, we were listening to, or watching the recorded media. The stream of indoctrination was constant.

Although being a Jehovah's Witness was very time consuming, we were supposed to be joyful about it. After all, we had **The Truth** and should be glad to be fed this fine "spiritual food" that could only be provided by the Faithful and Discreet Slave. To complain about any of it was viewed as an insult against Jehovah and The Organization.

Chapter 3
Jehovah's Witness Conventions

Besides the weekly meetings, The Organization would also arrange Jehovah's Witness conventions ("Assemblies") three times each year: Two Circuit Assemblies and one District Assembly for each geographical area. The Circuit Assembly was arranged for all the congregations within a circuit to attend. A District Assembly was bigger, as it consisted of a *group* of *circuits* in a geographical area.

Assemblies were very organized affairs: Every member of each congregation would be given an identification badge before each Assembly that was to be worn during the duration of the Assembly programs. The Assembly sites themselves were very orderly and well maintained: There would be a First Aid station on site, areas set aside to accommodate the elderly and handicapped, a clean-up committee, ushers, and, when I was younger, they even had food concession areas made available for breakfasts and lunches. Quite often we'd volunteer to help with the clean-up committee or the concession stands. The Clean-up committee ensured that the Assembly site would be left absolutely immaculate when finished. When I grew older they eventually did away with the concession stands due to the high cost of running them. It wasn't too much of a hardship though; it only meant that attendees needed to start bringing their own meals, or go out to a local restaurant for breakfast or lunch.

These Assemblies were designed as another avenue for mass indoctrination. However, they were different from the regular weekly meetings in several ways: *One*, They were primarily a *series* of sermons orated by various assigned brothers, *Two*, they usually included a drama or a primary skit *Three*, they usually featured an on-stage interview with ones especially strong in the faith, such as missionaries or a worker from Bethel, and *Four*, they always featured a mass baptism.

Although these items in the convention itinerary were meant to make Assemblies different from the routine weekly meetings, it still made for a long, tedious day; especially if you were young. There were no provisions for child care, as children were expected to sit through the day-long program with the parents; this even included babies.

In my area, the Circuit Assemblies were usually held once in the spring and once in the autumn. Up until I was a young adult, my congregation's circuit would meet in my hometown, Elmira, New York. Some of my very earliest memories include attending Circuit Assemblies at the Chemung County Fairgrounds in the grand stands. Later, as the population of members grew in the circuit, these Assemblies were re-located to the Elmira city armory building. Eventually the membership in the circuit grew so large that the Assemblies began being held at the local performing arts theater, the Samuel L. Clemens Center, in downtown Elmira. It was a very nice theater with cushy seats, a balcony, and a grand chandelier in the entrance. Next to it was a large public parking garage, so it was an ideal location for an Assembly.

I mainly remember the Circuit Assemblies at the Clemens Center. We'd start the program by nine in the morning and keep going until about four-something in the afternoon, with an hour and a half or so for a lunch break. Because our city was the host for our Circuit's Assemblies, our Kingdom Hall featured a baptismal pool installed in its basement. Since the theater we used for the Assemblies was located in the heart of Elmira's downtown, the lunch break afforded an opportunity to go out to lunch or do a little local site seeing. Elmira markets itself as "Mark Twain Country" due to the author's roots to the city. Woodlawn Cemetery held his grave, and Elmira College held Mark Twain's very own study room (which is an enclosed pavilion). There is also Riverside Park, which is a walk-through park built along the Chemung River spanning through Downtown. At that time, Elmira's downtown had plenty of places to eat, the Steele Memorial Library (which was pretty big), and places to shop. The Circuit Assemblies were good for the local economy.

When I was a young adult The Organization gave the green light for our district to build a Circuit Assembly hall in Henrietta, New York (about a two hour drive from Elmira). This Assembly Hall was made to replace all the venues that the various circuits in the district had been using. It was a very nice building: Pink marble flooring, Bible-themed murals, a coat check area, a large cafeteria, and it's own baptismal pool. With the completion of this Assembly hall, our Kingdom Hall no longer needed it's baptismal pool in the basement, so it was removed.

District Assemblies were much larger than Circuit Assemblies and lasted a few days. These required an arena, a convention center, or some other large venue to accommodate all the attendees. Every year, Dad and Mom took us to a different city for the District Assembly. We'd been to Syracuse, Utica, Binghamton, and several times we'd gone to Niagara Falls, and a few times we went to Rochester. On some occasions we'd travel back and forth daily, and on other occasions we'd stay the duration with a local Jehovah's Witness family.

All of these city's featured a nearby zoo, and sometimes Dad and Mom would take us to see the animals when the Assembly was finished. After starting the morning with a long road trip and sitting through a long Assembly program, the zoo was the perfect way to end the day!

On the occasions we went to Niagara Falls we'd make arrangements to stay the week with the Stevens family – a Jehovah's Witness family who lived on North Ogden Street in nearby Buffalo, New York. They had kids our ages, a big home and a big yard, so it was pretty nice. We always stayed an extra day or so longer than the Assembly so we could do some sight seeing and have a day to socialize with the Stevens'.

Lunch break at the Niagara Falls Assembly was always a treat! I loved the lunch breaks because the convention center was in the middle of the city, and we could walk to many of the tourist attractions. I still remember the multi-level greenhouse we'd visit – it was gorgeous! It had spiral staircases, tropical trees and plenty of lush foliage. Sometimes the bunch of us (my siblings and the Stevens' siblings) would walk across Rainbow bridge into Canada on our lunch breaks. And, of course, on our "tourist day" at the end of the Assembly, Dad and Mom would take us to Niagara Falls to visit all the remaining attractions – we always brought back lots of souvenirs each year!

On the years we went to Rochester, it was less exciting because Rochester wasn't as "tourist-y" as Niagara Falls, though it still had a few interesting attractions. The last time I attended the District Assembly in Rochester we camped out along the shores of Lake Ontario at Hamlin Beach. The weather was gorgeous, and I still remember the beautiful sunsets, the blue lake... on a clear day you could see all the way across to Canada on the other side. The year we stayed at Hamlin Beach was the year I was baptized into the faith; it was the summer of 1985 and I was seventeen years old.

Sometimes, The Organization would also arrange "International Conventions". These conventions were specially planned for anyone from any country to come to, and usually large enough to require a sports stadium in order to accommodate the number of delegates. In 1978 there the "Victorious Faith" International Convention in Pittsburgh, Pennsylvania that we attended. We stayed with another Jehovah's Witness family, the Woods, and they also had kids around our ages. The Assembly was held at Three Rivers Stadium. It wasn't as exciting as going to Niagara Falls, but still it was fun to meet a new family and make new friends.

Each Assembly had a biblical theme or slogan that set the tone for the information presented, Some of the presentations were interesting, and some were downright boring, but for the most part it always seemed like a long day, just sitting there listening and taking notes. One of the highlights of the District Assemblies was the yearly release of a new publication from The Watchtower Bible and Tract Society. It could be a new study book, or a pamphlet, or sometimes a cassette of re-mixed music from our Song Book. The new release was always met with a loud applause when it was announced.

Many times, especially at the District Assemblies, "apostates" would stand outside the convention location and try to hand us free Christian literature as we entered or left. Since Jehovah's Witnesses are firmly trained to reject anyone else's religious material, these "apostates" wouldn't get very far with us. We viewed them as enemies of God and didn't want anything to do with their "satanic" literature.

It took a lot of planning to attend a District Assembly, and Dad was a master at organization. He'd get the car tuned up and ready for the week-long venture. He kept in contact with our host family, had the trip mapped out, the rest stops planned out, and the funds planned out. Mom would make sure we all packed appropriate clothing in our suitcases, made sure we packed our bibles and made sure we had all our essentials: toothbrushes, combs, etc. With a family as large as ours, this was no small task! Then, early the next morning we'd all pile into the station wagon, with our luggage tied to the roof rack, and hit the road.

I don't know how us kids didn't drive Dad and Mom crazy on those trips! We were noisy, we bickered, we sang, we tried to talk over each other – it was nuts! I remember one time we were traveling down the highway, and Amelia and I were in the back seat that faced the tailgate, along with an overstuffed bag of our little brother's clothes. The tailgate window was down, causing some of the clothing to flap in the wind. Amelia thought it was kinda cool, so she tried to pull the clothes out just a bit more to see more flapping action – but somehow she pulled too hard and several articles of clothing were sucked out the tailgate window! Oh did we howl about that! Luckily, we were the only car on the road at that particular moment, so Dad pulled over to the shoulder of the road and went back to pick up the clothes – and gave her quite a tongue lashing for it!

One year, when I was fourteen, our family car was a Pacer, which we nick-named "The Bubble". By this time most of my older siblings had left home to venture life on their own, so a smaller family car was chosen. Since Pacers weren't the roomiest car, me and my older brother, Shane, took a commercial bus to the Stevens' home in Buffalo while the rest of the family went in the Pacer. I wasn't impressed with the bus ride; it was a long, boring trip with a bunch of strangers. I found myself wishing I was crammed in the family car with the rest of the family – and I'm sure that Shane probably felt the same way too!

Although the Assemblies always tended to be long, boring affairs, it was great to get out of town for a while and enjoy the tourist attractions. It was also nice to have the opportunity to meet other brothers and sisters in the faith and quite often we would become pen pals with them for a while. We always wrote to the kids in the Stevens' family, and Amelia also became pen pals with a Jehovah's Witness friend of the Stevens'. On another occasion, my brother, Joe, met a lovely Canadian sister at an Assembly in Rochester; they became pen pals, and a year later he moved to Canada and married her.

For me, Assemblies were always a mixed blessing: On the one hand I got to get a break from the routine, go someplace different, and meet new people. On the *other* hand, it still included a long boring trip to sit through a long boring series of sermons (though I did like the dramas and skits). And by the time I grew into my teen years, I always felt sorry for the young children who had to sit still throughout the program, reading their Watchtower Society published "My Book Of Bible Stories" for the thousandth time as the program droned on. I was pretty sure many of those kids must have had the book memorized, considering it was the most child-friendly book that the Watchtower Society was publishing at the time. Oh sure, some parents were nice enough to provide their children with a notepad and pencil to draw with, but that only worked until a certain age. By the time a child was old enough to read, the child was expected to take notes on the material presented at the series of talks just like the adults did.

In spite of my misgivings though, I still wholeheartedly believed in the Jehovah's Witness doctrine, and always felt a twinge of guilt for feeling so bored with the program.

Chapter 4
Jehovah's Witness Baptisms

The main event at each Assembly was the scheduled mass baptism. Since Assemblies are the *only* times that the Jehovah's Witnesses perform baptisms, it is always an event with many baptismal candidates; usually numbering several dozen in the Circuit Assemblies, and easily numbering up to a couple hundred in the District Assemblies.

In order to be recognized as an official member of the Jehovah's Witnesses, you must be baptized into the faith. It doesn't matter if you have been previously baptized by a different Christian denomination, you must have a *Jehovah's Witness* baptism in order to be an official member of the congregation. Jehovah's Witnesses believe that baptism is actually a dedication to God, not a symbol of repentance and forgiveness of sin. Since they don't feel other denominations in Christendom are dedicated to God, they do not recognize those baptisms as valid.

The process for baptism is lengthy. First, you tell one of your Elders that you want to get baptized. He confers with the other Elders as to whether they think you are ready for such a step. They consider how long you've been associating with the congregation, your age, and your current reputation. If they decide you are ready, they make arrangements with you for a series of question-and-answer sessions. These sessions consist of *several dozen* questions, specified by The Organization, all pertaining to Jehovah's Witness doctrine. In my own personal experience, one of the Elders would come to my house to meet with me once per week, spending about an hour each time, going over the baptismal questions with me. Questions all pertained to Jehovah's Witness doctrine. You must answer the questions correctly *according to the Jehovah's Witness doctrine*, otherwise they will not consider you to be eligible for baptism. Of course, this process is in complete contrast with Bible accounts of baptism, in which a person simply needed to show faith in Christ in order to be eligible for baptism. At the time, however, I didn't see that. I simply went along with whatever The Organization directed.

When you've successfully finished the series of question sessions, you simply needed to wait until the next Assembly. At the Assembly you'd be handed an itinerary for the program at the door, which would include the day and time the mass baptism was to be performed. Females were to wear a modest, one-piece bathing suit, and males were to wear a white tee-shirt with their swim trunks, as Jehovah's Witnesses practice immersion-only baptism.

That's right, immersion-only; it doesn't matter what your physical condition is, every single part of your body must be briefly submerged, period. If any part of your body remained out of the water the baptism wasn't considered valid and you'd have to be re-submerged. People who are wheelchair bound, or very weak (such as the elderly) are typically carried into, and out of the baptismal pool. As for members with tracheostomies (a permanent hole in the throat through which a person breathes), immersion baptism presents a unique problem of its own: I remember a brother in my home congregation, Ward, who had a tracheostomy. In order to be baptized by immersion, Ward would need to seal up the hole, and if the seal accidentally broke or leaked, water would rush in through the neck hole and drown him. Immersion baptism was a matter of life or death to him – he was terrified of it! Because he feared for his life, it took several tries before he was successfully baptized into the faith.

Imagine being terrified for your immediate life by the very act of being baptized! Although I agree with immersion baptism in general, I also believe that God is merciful enough to allow alternative forms of baptisms in these kinds of situations. God doesn't want to terrorize us – couldn't Ward get *mostly* submerged instead? I didn't understand why they had to be so rigid in Ward's case, he had an unusual circumstance. But who was I to question the Elders about it. They were my spiritual leaders and I had no right to question them.

On the day of a scheduled baptism, there would be a special talk regarding baptism just before the lunch break (because the baptisms take place during the long lunch break). All baptismal candidates are invited to come to the Baptismal Seating Area directly in front of the speaker's platform in order to hear this talk, as the talk is specifically directed towards them. The talk reviews the meaning of baptism (according to Jehovah's Witness doctrine), the responsibilities of membership, and the warnings of becoming a target for Satan once you've been baptized. After that, a prayer would be offered up, a baptismal praise would be sung from the Song Book, and then the entire convention would be dismissed for lunch. The baptismal candidates would immediately retreat to a changing area and line up for their immersion at the pool.

In our Circuit Assembly Hall, the baptismal pool is a permanent structure built right into the building. For District Assemblies, the brothers usually brought in a large, above-ground pool that would be dismantled after the Assembly was finished. The pools were located in such a way as to have plenty of space around them for spectators. It's a big event that family and friends wanted to share, and so there would be many people taking photographs and applauding the ones being baptized.

Baptism into the faith totally changes your position within the congregation. Before you are baptized you are allowed to do the door to door work and take part in the Theocratic Ministry School skits, but nothing more. *After* baptism, you were automatically considered to be an ordained minister in the faith, no matter who you were. As such, a baptized member could sign up to be a Pioneer (a particular rank of evangelizers) or accept a Missionary assignment if he or she desired. The males could also earn *special* privileges, such as becoming a Ministerial Servant, an Elder, a literature attendant (for ordering the material for the studies), run the microphones during meetings, etc. Females didn't generally receive other *special* privileges after baptism.

Another change that came with baptism was your fellowshipping status. Once you were baptized, you were considered as a good spiritual influence on others. If you remained unbaptized, especially when you've been associating with the Witnesses for a long time, people would start questioning your motives. To remain unbaptized after having full knowledge of "The Truth" was simply unheard of. In many cases, members of the congregation will start pulling away from you, imagining that in some way you aren't an ideal person to associate with. Although they don't actually shun you, you'll start noticing that you are receiving less invitations to events and gatherings.

This was one of the reasons I eventually decided to get baptized. You see, I was *born and raised* into the faith, and here I was, seventeen years old and *not* baptized yet. Most of my siblings got baptized before they were seventeen. And everyone started noticing that I wasn't baptized yet. Oh, they were nice about it...mostly it was "friendly" questioning: Hey Tami, are you gonna get baptized at the next Assembly?". My mother started feeling the pressure from everyone, and so even she started asking me about it. They all figured that, after 17 years of being "in The Truth", surely I must be ready for baptism! The District Assembly was months away, but I was hearing the questions, and the closer to Assembly time, the more frequently the questions were coming.

I knew I wasn't ready for baptism. At the time, I secretly had a "worldly" boyfriend who I wasn't willing to surrender ("worldly" simply means a non-Jehovah's Witness). I was also young and unsettled, I knew it was too soon for me. Being baptized would mean reigning myself in, breaking up with the boyfriend, and being pressured into Pioneering (I was *not* cut out for the door-to-door work!). But of course, I couldn't tell anyone these things: First of all, the whole boyfriend thing would mark me as a bad association in the congregation, and that meant nobody would ever invite me to do anything anymore. The second issue was that it is considered a weakness in faith to loathe the door-to-door evangelizing. And, of course, such a weakness would also mark me as a bad association as well. I was between a rock and a hard place. Finally, I gave in and prepared for baptism, just to get everyone off my back. I didn't want to fight it tooth and nail, after all I *did* sincerely believe in all of the Jehovah's Witness doctrine at the time. So, that summer, in July of 1985, I was baptized into the Jehovah's Witness faith at a District Assembly in Rochester, New York.

I wasn't the only one in my congregation getting baptized at that particular Assembly; there were identical twin sisters about my age who I was friends with who were also getting baptized, as well as another younger girl. I was glad that I wasn't the only one in my congregation getting baptized; I didn't want a lot of attention directed on me in my home congregation.

The actual baptism itself went rather quickly. Males and females went to separate changing areas. In my changing area there were some sisters in the faith there waiting for us in order to help us with with our buttons and zippers and things. Once we all got lined up at the pool, it was just a matter of waiting your turn to step into the water, get dunked, and step back out. With each immersion, spectators around the pool would flash their cameras and applaud. Stationed next to the pool was a brother in the faith who'd hold your towel for you as you stepped into the water. Back at the changing area the sisters would help us dry off and get back into our buttons and zippers again.

Once you are baptized into the faith, there is no turning back: You either behave as a proper Jehovah's Witness or you get congregational discipline. After baptism, if you change your mind and decide that the Jehovah's Witness lifestyle really isn't your "thing", you are perceived as an enemy of Jehovah and nobody in the congregation will have anything to do with you. Therefore, deciding to be baptized was a very important decision. But like I said before, although I didn't feel ready for the baptism, I *did* accept all of the doctrines at the time, so I wasn't worried that I'd change my mind later.

That would come back to haunt me years later.

Chapter 5
The Memorial

Another unique thing in the Jehovah's Witness world is their version of the Communion Supper, which they call "The Memorial", or "The Lord's Evening Meal". They gather to commemorate this event only once per year; on the Hebrew calendar date of Nisan 14th, after sundown. Although Jehovah's Witnesses are not Messianic Jews, they hold to that date because it is the date that Jesus Christ ate the Last Supper with his twelve apostles. They hold the event only once per year because they view it as an anniversary, and anniversaries are observed only once per year.

Jehovah's Witnesses are extremely particular about their Memorial emblems: The wine must be red wine and not grape juice, and without any additives (can't have additives such as spices, fruit juice, etc.), and the bread must not have any leavening agent in it. This is in line with the wine and unleavened bread that Jesus ate with his disciples.

They are also very selective on who can accept the wine and the bread ("partaking"). Remember, in the Jehovah's Witness doctrine, only 144,000 believers will go to heaven (the heavenly hope) while all the remaining ones will stay on a paradise earth (the earthly hope). The ones with the heavenly hope, also known as "the anointed", "the remnant" or "the chosen", will be co-rulers with Christ over the ones with the earthly hope. This is all based on The Organization's erroneous interpretation of prophecy in the books of Isaiah and Revelation. According to their interpretation, only the ones with the heavenly hope are in the New Covenant with Jesus Christ, and thus are the only ones who can partake of the emblems. As for the members with an earthly hope, they aren't in the New Covenant; their salvation is dependent upon their association with the ones in the New Covenant. In essence this means that they believe Jesus Christ mediates for the anointed ones going to heaven, and the anointed ones mediate for those staying on Earth. (*The Watchtower, February 15, 1991, p. 17 para.. 8 and p. 18, para. 11, Insight On the Scriptures, Volume 2, p. 362 "Mediator" (1993), The Watchtower, March 15, 2004 pp.5-6)*

Since Jehovah's Witnesses believe that God has been choosing ones for the heavenly hope since the beginning of Christianity, there are less than 10,000 Jehovah's Witnesses in the world who partake of the emblems (though the membership numbers over seven million globally).

This doctrine is indirectly related to their baptism doctrine: Remember, in the Jehovah's Witness world baptism is a symbol of dedication to God, even though scripture actually states that baptism is in symbol of forgiveness through Christ (Acts 2:38). This is because, in the Jehovah's Witness doctrine, "baptism into Christ's death" is only for the 144,000 – not the general membership of the denomination, which they base on the passage at Romans 6:3. Because they teach a distinction of one group being heaven-bound and another group being earth-bound, they have to revamp the doctrine of baptism to fit these teachings. Therefore, because *all* members must be baptized, they teach baptism as a dedication to God, leaving the "baptism into Christ" concept set apart for the 144,000. *The Watchtower, February 15, 1998, page 14, paragraph 11, The Watchtower, July 1 1998, page 17 paragraph 14 United In Worship book, Chapter 12 paragraphs 6-8*

It's difficult to explain how one gets "chosen" for the heavenly hope. Basically, the brother or sister in the faith somehow realizes that he or she will be going to heaven instead of living on the paradise earth (a.k.a. "The New Order"). The member then speaks to the Elders in the congregation in an attempt to confirm the validity of the realization. If, after speaking with the Elders and attempting scriptural guidance this person still believes he or she is a "chosen one", the Elders agree to let the person partake of the emblems.

At every Memorial event around the world, the Elders of the congregations count how many partake of the emblems and report the numbers to The Organization. If the Elders do not believe the brother or sister is a chosen one, yet the person partakes of the emblems anyway, the Elders will refuse to count that person. They also won't count a partaker who is not baptized, is simply a non-believing visitor, or is disfellowshipped (excommunicated) from the faith.

Once in a while, a congregation will get a newly baptized member who believes he or she is chosen and thus partakes; and later this person realizes that he/she was not really chosen after all. This is viewed as an honest mistake that Jehovah will forgive. However, if you actually know you aren't chosen, and yet you partake anyway, it is viewed as a grave sin.

I had never felt the call as a "chosen one" when I was a Jehovah's Witness, so I never had to worry about the issue myself. In the congregation I grew up in though, we had three partakers; one was a married brother in the faith, and the other two were married sisters in the faith. I remember wondering, each year as I saw them partake, how their families must feel about them leaving them behind to to go to heaven instead of being together in the New Order. I remember hoping that, if I ever married, that my husband wouldn't be taken away from me like that. But that wasn't a thought that you voiced because you were supposed to be *happy* for those who were chosen; after all, it was the highest honor a human could receive!

Having "anointed ones" in your congregation made things interesting. Such ones were looked upon as extra-cool-spiritual. They were held in higher esteem than the common members of the congregation, and often were given special privileges due to their spiritual status. Although female anointeds still didn't get to be an Elder or Ministerial Servant, they were still more respected when they had anything to say. Common members tended to treat the anointeds with a little more respect and wanted to be their friends.

During the time I was a Jehovah's Witness, it was taught that the New Testament was written primarily for the anointed ones, and therefore only the anointed were able to understand it. Later though, some time after I left the Jehovah's Witnesses, the doctrine was tweaked to mean that only the anointed *in Watchtower Society's Worldwide Headquarters* understood the scriptures properly (after all, they were Jehovah's channel of communication on earth). Basically, this means that, according to Jehovah's Witness doctrine, only the Governing Body in Bethel has the correct understanding of scripture.

Since The Memorial is considered to be the holiest night of the year for Jehovah's Witnesses, members are expected to invite non-Witness friends, family, neighbors, and co-workers to the event. As a result, the Kingdom Hall was always packed each year. When our congregation had to split due to overgrowth, we had to share the Kingdom Hall on that same night: Two observances – one just after sundown, and another a couple of hours later. Our congregations took turns each year as to who got the early one and who got the later one.

There was always a lot of preparation for this most special event: We had special Bible reading passages to read throughout the weeks leading up to The Memorial. Volunteers from the congregation would also make a special effort to clean the Kingdom Hall from top to bottom, making sure it was presentable to all the extra visitors. On the night of the event, some of the brothers in the congregation would volunteer as parking attendants. Their duties were to ensure efficient parking and safe traffic flow to accommodate all the extra visitors that were coming. Members dressed up a little better than usual, and even the babies had on little suits and frilly dresses. This event was so important that, if you were too sick to attend this observance, the Elders would arrange to come to your home and give you an at-home Memorial observance. Inside the Kingdom Hall, several extra rows of chairs would be set up, and on the stage area would be a table set with a bottle of wine, wine glasses, and plates of unleavened bread.

The Memorial Talk was pretty much the same thing each year: There would be some reading of the related Bible scriptures, but a large portion of the Talk would be spent on indoctrination: Explanations on the who's and why's of partaking, the differences between the heavenly hope and the earthly hope, and their version of what the New Covenant is all about. These doctrinal explanations were necessary since there would be so many non-Witness visitors in amongst us those nights; they didn't want these visitors to unknowingly "sin" by partaking of the emblems. The wine would be poured into the wine glasses, and the attendees would pass the glass from one to another until the entire number attending had an opportunity to pass the glass. Next, the plate of unleavened bread would be passed from one attendee to the next just like with the wine. Only the anointed ones were allowed to actually take a sip of the wine and a bite of the bread. Most congregations have no "chosen ones" in them, therefore *nobody* partakes in those congregations. After these rituals were completed, we'd sing an appropriate praise from our song book and be dismissed.

Missing the Memorial was something to be avoided at all costs. Members were to ensure they could get the time off from their employment, and even disfellowshipped (excommunicated) members seeking reinstatement were expected to show up. If you were newly studying with a Jehovah's Witness, you were expected to come to the Memorial with the member who was studying with you. If your car didn't work or you had a broken leg, you were expected to call one of the members in the congregation for a ride to the event.. Therefore, every year, the Elders would pre-arrange transportation for the very elderly members who were living in nursing homes.

It was the one event of the year that a devout Jehovah's Witness wouldn't miss for anything.

Chapter 6
Public Evangelism

I think the most common thing that Jehovah's Witnesses are known for is their door-to-door evangelism, a.k.a. "Field Service". This activity is expected of every member who is mentally and physically able to do so. They consider "going out in Service" to be a life-saving work for those who aren't believers: therefore, one who slacks off on this duty is often considered to be spiritually weak and lacking brotherly love towards their fellow humans. Service is also often considered to be one of the charitable works they perform. The point of Field Service is to find "sheep-like ones" who want to start a personal Bible study program. A Bible study is actually a personal book study, as we were instructed to teach them using the Watchtower Society publications, with the Bible as a mere reference tool for the studies.

Let me give you a little background on this duty: First, all evangelizing members in the congregation are called "Publishers". Whether you are part of the rank and file, or are a Ministerial Servant, or an Elder, you are a Publisher. If you are not yet baptized, you are specified as being an "Unbaptized Publisher". In order to be an Unbaptized Publisher, you must have a record of consistent, frequent association with the congregation for several months and currently have a clean reputation. The Elders confer together as to your association with the congregation and your reputation before deeming you eligible to be an Unbaptized Publisher. In the normal course of things, you aren't allowed to get baptized as a member of the congregation unless you become an Unbaptized Publisher first (unless you have mental or physical limitations to prevent you from this duty). Although Saturdays were considered to be "Magazine Days" (in which you offered people the *The Watchtower* and *Awake!* magazines), the week days were set aside for offering other literature. Each month a different literature offer was presented. The Kingdom Ministry Sheet always announced which literature offering we were to have each month. We were to obey that direction each month, and the congregations always made sure to have enough of the current literature on hand for participants to offer in their door-to-door service.

Service meetings were the venue for organizing the door-to-door work. Basically, the place you met for the Tuesday book study was the same place you met for the Service meetings . There were "Service Conductors" who conducted the service meetings.

A service meeting basically went by this format: Everyone gathers at the meeting place a few minutes before the scheduled time. There is a few minutes of fellowshipping while waiting for everyone to arrive. At the appointed time, everyone gets seated, the Service Conductor speaks a few words of commencement, and then leads the group in a short prayer. Next, the Conductor reads the Daily Text devotional, and allows the other members in the group to make any comments that they wish regarding the devotional; but only for a short amount of time. Then, the Conductor inquires as to whether any of the attendees have already made Service arrangements. (Many times, members will plan to go out in service together, or in groups, or in specific areas of town). Arrangements weren't a requirement, but they were a common thing. For those who didn't happen to plan prior arrangements, the Conductor would make sure those ones would have a plan for grouping and territory before sending everyone out into the "Field" in their car groups. Once the arrangements were made, the Service Conductor would offer a closing prayer and everyone would head out to their assigned areas.

These meetings only lasted for about half an hour. In spite of their rigid formula, these were more flexible than any other meeting because the participants could invent their own amount of service hours per day; there was no set amount of time that a participant was required to be out in service for. If you wanted to go out for only one hour that was okay, and if you wanted to go out for more than that, it was still okay.

Participants were also free to decide which area they wanted to work in, and decide whether they wanted to "work" established bible-studies they've already started with non-believers, or return to the "not-at-homes" they encountered on a previous day of Service.

Formally going out in service involved "Territories". To understand a "Territory" you need to realize that each particular congregation was responsible for a specific geographical area. Each congregation's geographical area was divided up into smaller sections which were called "Territories". The congregation would print out small maps of each territory so that members could "take out" a Territory for the service work. A person was expected to keep the territory for a certain amount of time before turning it back in for someone else to use. This helped ensure that a territory wouldn't be overcrowded with too many evangelizers at any given time. Members were instructed to never to go out in service outside of their specific territories because doing so could encroach upon the geographical area of another congregation.

When one takes out a territory, one is expected to "cover" it before returning it. "Covering" it meant speaking to every person within that territory. A territory fell under various categories: residential (homes), rurals (countryside and farmland), business territory (places of business and employment) and street-witnessing (standing on the street corner speaking to passers-by). Of course, sometimes there were obstacles to this: Some communities have a "no canvassing" rule – especially in places like mobile home parks or condominiums. In such cases, the brothers of the congregation would procure the address and/or telephone numbers of those who lived in those places and make up new kinds of "territory": Letter Writing Territories and Telephone Territories. If someone took out the Letter Writing territory, the duty was to write doctrinal letters to all of the addressees. If someone took out a telephone territory, the duty was to call everyone on the list and engage them in a doctrinal conversation.

I didn't have too much of a problem with the Letter Writing territories: Letters aren't all that invasive; addressees can read them at their own convenience and they aren't pressured to respond in any way. But the Telephone Territories were another story. Since I myself would be *very* uncomfortable if a stranger obtained my home phone number and tried to preach to me over the phone, I couldn't bring myself to inflict that upon someone else.

There was only one time when I was duped into being with a Telephone Territory group; basically, I wasn't told what we were doing until *after* all the other car groups had left for their territories. I was simply told that our territory was "a little bit of everywhere". I took that to mean we were going to drive around trying to find the "not-at-homes" from a previous Service day. NOPE! Turned out that it was Telephone Territory. Ugh! There were just of few of us altogether, and everyone took turns calling a number and speaking to whomever answered. Everyone took turns, and I continued to refuse politely whenever my turn was up. I just couldn't bring myself to do it, no matter how much they tried to talk me into it. I'm sure I made a terrible impression on them that day, but I didn't care, I was much too uncomfortable with it. After that experience, I always made sure I knew *exactly* which territory I was working in.

Participants almost always went door-to-door by twos. Once in a while a brother would be willing to go to a door alone, but that was only in the secure neighborhoods where the risk of personal danger was very minimal. Sisters always went to doors together. And children were always in tow with the parents; even babies in strollers.

All Publishers are expected to go out in service on a regular basis. This means, at the very least, once per month; preferably more if your circumstances allow for it. Conducting a home Bible study with your own children was also counted as "service", allowing busy and single mothers to count time per month. At the end of each month, every publisher must fill out a monthly time slip to document the amount of hours they spent in service for that month. This slip of paper required a Publisher to document how many hours they spent evangelizing throughout the month, how many Bible studies they scheduled or started, and how many items of literature they "placed" (gave to non-believers). If a Publisher does not submit a paper each month for at least six months straight, they are labeled as an "irregular publisher", and immediate action is taken to encourage the member to perform more Field Service.

Some members like to take their Publisher status a bit further, and apply for the level of "Pioneer". A Pioneer is a Publisher who goes out in Service on a full-time basis. Becoming a Pioneer gives that member a special status in the congregation, and others tend to look up to them with a little more respect, as they must be more spiritual than the rank and file Publishers. There were three levels of Pioneering: Auxiliary Pioneer, Regular Pioneer, and Special Pioneer. Each successive level was responsible for a certain amount of hours spent in Field Service each month. To become a Pioneer you would have to submit an application form. The Elders would review your application, and confer regarding your reputation and your perceived spiritual "health", and make a decision as whether to accept your application. You could choose to pioneer once in a while, or you could choose to do it on a continual basis. Although I never applied to be a Pioneer, other members of my family frequently applied to do so on various occasions.

If plain ol' pioneering wasn't enough, a member could become a missionary. Missionaries are usually chosen by invitation only, and were basically members who were sent to foreign countries to pioneer. If a member accepted the invitation he or she would first be sent to the Gilead School. The Gilead School runs two sessions each year, with each session running for about five months. At Gilead, the students learn the languages they needed to know as well as the local customs of the areas they were being sent to. They are also taught special techniques for establishing Bible studies, since that was the main purpose of the mission. Originally, the

Gilead School was established in South Lansing, New York, though later it was moved to Patterson, New York. Although I've seen missionaries as guest speakers and interviewees at assemblies, I didn't personally know any of them.

As a Publisher or Pioneer goes out in service, they bring along their service record sheet. This is a pocket-sized sheet of paper in which they keep track of the addresses of which homes they've visited, which homes were "not at homes", and any literature they placed, and any other special comments needed ("elderly woman", "married couple", "ex-Catholic" etc.). This record was for their own personal use to help them remember such details the next time they went to visit the people listed on the sheet.

Members of the congregation quietly notice how often other members go out in service. If they notice you are not going out so often, they try to encourage you, and there are ways that they do that. Sometimes, one will privately tell you they've noticed your lack of hours and ask if he or she can help you in some way: Transportation, child care, etc. Sometimes, a member will simply start inviting you to go out in service with him or her on a particular day. Sometimes, the Elders will notice your absence in the Service and try to remind you, nicely, of your biblical duty to go out.

Now, I get that some people are totally at ease with going door-to-door to preach, and that's fine for them. I have no problem with that. *HOWEVER*, some of us are much more comfortable with less direct approaches. I was not ashamed of my faith, I simply wasn't comfortable with the feeling of invading somebody's day with my religion when they didn't ask for it. Especially on a sunny Saturday when people already had their chores and weekend plans in order. I always thought it was better to leave an open invitation for anyone who may be interested. Actions such as quietly reading my Bible in the break room at work and letting a natural conversation take its course, or simply leaving a restaurant tip inside a religious tract with my contact information, would have worked much better for me.

Although indirect approaches were acceptable, it was an expectation that a member in good standing would be going out in the door-to-door service on a regular basis. The basic idea was that you must show love towards others, and this was to be shown by coming to their doorsteps and offering Christian Truth to them. Not matter which other ways you preached to people, the door-to-door service was a *must* if you were physically able.

You never knew who you were going to encounter at the door until it happened. Now, most of the time it was either a "not-at-home" or someone who simply was not interested in what we had to say. But once in a while, you got a surprise – sometimes in a good way, and sometimes in a bad way.

For example, I got a good surprise one time, shortly after my baptism: I came to a door, the weather was nice, and the woman was sitting on her porch. She was nice enough, but not very interested. Then I hear the distinctive voice of a child that I had worked with at a summer daycare the year before – and I looked up and saw him; Shawn Smith, along with his little sister, Mary. Those two were such a joy to work with the previous year, and I was glad to see them! He came and gave me a big ol' bear hug (at least, from a nine-year-old's point of view), and his mother just beamed. It was a wonderful moment that I'll never forget!

And then there's the time I got a bad surprise: Later that same year, I was going door-to-door with Rebecca, an older sister from the congregation. It was my turn to present the literature offering to the householder. I did great on my presentation – I delivered my quick introduction flawlessly and engaged him in a conversation that easily segued into my literature. I thought I had the deal sealed...until I had to look down to get the literature out of my tote bag for him. It was at that point that I realized his pants were unzipped...and "he" was hanging out. OH MY! In spite of my young age (merely 17 years old), I immediately decided to act as though I didn't notice, and kept going with my presentation as usual. The man graciously took the literature, and politely excused himself.

We *very* willingly let him excuse himself, and we walked away. Once we got out of earshot, Rebecca asked how I was feeling. I let her know I was a bit shocked, but okay. Then she expressed how well I handled it; and apparently she couldn't decide whether I had noticed his "deal", which is why she asked. I was grateful for the confirmation that I concealed it so well, since I didn't want the guy to know his harassment worked. *HOWEVER*, I wasn't eager for such a surprise to happen again!

A zealous Publisher could feasibly go out in service every day of the week if he or she wanted to, as there were always a service meeting one could attend (you weren't required to stick with just your book study group). This was especially helpful for those who were Pioneering. Members were always encouraged to "do more" if they could. Going out in service was considered the most important thing we could do as Christians. Very often, in our regular weekly Bible meetings we were admonished to do more if we could.

The main goal was to start "Bible Studies" with the unbelievers. Of course, the "Bible Studies" weren't strictly Bible studies, as the primary base of the studies always included the prescribed literature published by the Watchtower Society. I wasn't very good at the door-to-door work; although I could succeed in placing my literature some days, I never was able to drum up an actual Bible study.

In many cases, members also made plans to go out in Service even on holidays such as Christmas or Thanksgiving, as this was something strongly encouraged by The Organization.

Our Kingdom Ministry, *November 1979 p. 2 Announcements*
Our Kingdom Ministry, *December 1987, p. 2 para. 5*

When I became old enough to think it through, I discovered that I didn't like the idea of going house to house on the holidays. Even though we were encouraged to start later in the day during the holidays (to allow the non-believers their "sleep in" time) I realized that these non-believers still used these holidays as family times. I didn't feel right about interrupting them, even though I didn't believe in their holidays. My thinking was that, by being respectful of their "space", it would help them be more open to us when we came to their doors on other days. Therefore, I began to refrain from the Service work on holidays.

Another version of Service was called "Informal" or "Incidental" witnessing". This was the most easiest way to evangelize because it didn't take any kind of preparation or planning. I was much better as Incidental Witnessing than I was at the formal Field Service. Basically, Incidental Witnessing happened on the fly. If you saw someone on the bus reading a newspaper, you could use the news to segue into a conversation about God and His plan to rid the world of evil. If you were reading your Bible on a park bench and someone else came along, you could start a Bible conversation then as well. Sometimes, friends and neighbors who knew you might ask you a few questions about your beliefs, in which case you can begin a good conversation then too. There was always opportunities to "witness" to someone in an unplanned setting. And yes, the time spent in informal witnessing was countable on the monthly time slips.

Those time slips were considered to be a very important piece of documentation. It helped show your spiritual fervor, helped identify the spiritual health of the congregation, and showed an individual Publisher's obedience to The Organization. In essence, these slips of paper were a measure of your spirituality. To willfully disregard your monthly time slip worked against the Unity of the Organization, and and was viewed as a signal of one's failing spirituality. Therefore, the Elders would be sure to give you a phone call if you "forgot" to turn in your time slip on any given month. If you couldn't recall having any time put in for the month, oftentimes an Elder would insist that you must have talked to *someone* about God during the month, and write you down for at least an hour's worth in the month. They didn't like to have publishers shown with zero time.

The reporting of time slips was so important that the Watchtower Society would publish articles regarding the importance of doing so from time to time. For example, the **Our Kingdom Ministry Sheet** of December, 2002, in the article titled *"Do You Contribute to an Accurate Report?"*, it likened the reporting of one's time to the biblical accounts of when God's people specifically recorded the numbers of things. They also claimed that an accurate report was an encouragement to the brotherhood and a display of one's respect for Jehovah's arrangement. The basic idea was that, if you didn't faithfully turn in your monthly time reports, you were neglecting the brotherhood and disrespecting God.

Towards the end of my membership with the Jehovah's Witnesses, those time slips became something I grew to dislike, and for a few months before I broke away from the sect I stopped reporting my time. Oh, I still did the door-to-door work and incidental witnessing, I just wasn't reporting the numbers anymore. I began to see that it was a matter of being a slave to numbers and a slave to appearances. I grew to realize that my worth wasn't dependent on those time slips – God knew what I was doing, shouldn't that be all that counts? To have my spiritual status hinge on a number seemed shallow and unbiblical. I explained this to the elders when I made my decision to stop handing in my monthly slips. They let it slide for a few months, but then I got the phone call wanting the numbers for those months. I told them I didn't keep track, reminding them of my reasons, and told them I didn't know how many hours I put in for each month. So they guesstimated a number and put it in their records anyway.

Although failing to report one's Field Service time was not exactly considered to be a crime, it was definitely something that a "true worshiper" would not neglect. In the Jehovah's Witness world, obedience to The Organization is the same as obedience to Jehovah God, therefore a devout member would be sure to obediently turn in their time each month.

Chapter 7
Recreational Activities

Although the Jehovah's Witnesses do not have weekly fellowship groups like most churches do, they still hold recreational events several times each year. This would include picnics, inter-congregational gatherings, wedding showers, baby showers, and various other events. Of course, we were always reminded to keep these events "clean", and to be sure to avoid bringing reproach upon Jehovah during our gatherings: Don't disturb any neighbors, keep the event area free of litter, no excessive consumption of alcohol, avoid questionable music, avoid "worldly" association, etc.

Every summer our Elders organized a congregational picnic. Living in Elmira, there were plenty of great places to choose for having these picnics: Harris Hill, which is known as the Soaring Capitol of the World, was always a favorite picnic spot. On sunny days the Gliders would be towed out, one right after the other, to lazily ride the convection currents. There was plenty of scenic views of the Chemung Valley below, lots of woodland trails, a public swimming pool, a golf area, playgrounds, children's rides and even a souvenir shop. Then there was Sullivan's Monument, a state park a few miles outside of Elmira. It was built in honor of General Sullivan, who campaigned against the Iroquois Indians in the late 1700's. This park boasted a towering pillar that was the monument, a large wooded picnic grounds, a pavilion, hiking trails and ball fields. On other occasions we'd go to a public park, such as Grove Park on the north side of Elmira. It had trees, a big grassy area, a playground, public pool, basketball court, and a large enclosed picnic pavilion. Other times we'd go to Eldridge Park, which was an amusement park complete with a wooden roller coaster, Merry-Go-Round, haunted house, paddle boats, teacup rides, concession stands, game booths and a large family picnic area. It also boasted a large pond that was a favorite fishing spot for the locals.

These congregation picnics were always a blast! We'd all bring a dish to share and play whatever kinds of games people brought: Baseball, badminton, volleyball, Frisbee, etc. Kids would play tag, adults would chit chat, some would play lawn games such as croquet or horseshoes – everyone always enjoyed these gatherings. Quite often someone would bring a guitar and some of us would sit around singing folk songs and worship songs. We'd always come home exhausted but very happy.

Sometimes, during the winter, other group activities would be organized: I remember one February, when I was a young teenager, they organized an inter-congregational dance party. They rented a large public hall and invited members from other Kingdom Halls in our circuit. We had all kinds of good music, lots of food, and everybody got to meet new people, it was wonderful! I looked a few years older than my real age, and found myself being invited to dance by young brothers from other congregations. For an awkward teen who didn't like how she looked, that was the highlight of my evening! On another occasion, a married couple in the congregation invited everyone to their home in the country for a sledding party. They had LOTS of space, a perfect hill for sledding, and plenty of hot chocolate and warm food. On yet another occasion, the congregation rented a public hall and organized a congregational talent show, complete with folk music, bible skits, and puppet shows, it was very entertaining. Yeah, these congregational get-togethers have always brought happy memories!

Aside from these congregational gatherings, members often times had other social events. For example, since Jehovah's Witnesses don't celebrate birthdays or holidays, my mother would organize a "Sharing Party" for the congregation's kids once in while. There would be cake, ice cream, soda pop, party games, decorations, and party favors. It looked just like a regular birthday party, only it wasn't for anyone's birthday, and each child that came received a gift. I carried on that tradition in my adult life, and organized "Just Because" parties for my own children as well.

Adults would also organize in-home gatherings for the grown-ups: Tupperware parties, candle parties, wedding showers, baby showers, and wedding anniversary parties, to name a few. Since I grew up in a large congregation, we always had opportunities for get-togethers and recreational association. Quite often a host or hostess would invite the bible-study students that members found in the door-to-door work, in order to show them that Jehovah's Witnesses do *indeed* have fun throughout the year.

Sometimes members would organize a "happy" event to bolster a member who has suffered a tragedy. I remember one year our Witness friend, Sue, was abandoned by her husband, leaving her a single mother with two young children just a few weeks before their sixth wedding anniversary. Sue was a really nice person and we hated to see her hurting so my sister, Laurel, organized an all-female surprise gathering for Sue on her anniversary date so that she wouldn't be left alone feeling rejected on that day. Sue, of course, was unaware of these surprise plans and called me on the phone a few days before the event to invite me over to her place on that day because she didn't want to be alone on her anniversary. What could I say? I didn't have the heart to refuse her offer without explaining the upcoming plans, so I simply laughed and said "Well...Sue, you already have something going on that day, you just don't know it yet". She laughed, mock-complaining how she ruined her own surprise, and I could tell she was glad that others were thinking of her in her plight. In spite of the loss of the surprise factor, she had a great time with us on the day of the gathering: Food, games, desserts, fun, laughing, camaraderie – it was exactly what she needed to lift her mood!

My sister Laurel was always good at considering the needs of others like that. I remember another time, when I was hosting a Home & Garden party at my home for the sisters of the congregation: It was just two days before the party when Laurel called me on the telephone. She informed me that an ex-member of the congregation, Kay, had just been reinstated into the fold, and asked if she could bring Kay along for the party too. Apparently Kay had been out of the loop for about twenty years, so she didn't have anyone in the congregation that she knew. I thought it was a great idea – not only could Kay start feeling accepted right away, but this would be the perfect opportunity for her to start getting to know the other sisters in the congregation. Of course I would make room on my guest list for one more person! Laurel was such a sweetie.

Although being a Jehovah's Witness meant avoiding holidays and birthdays, I didn't mind because there were so many other opportunities for fun and fellowship. Later, when I moved to other cities and began attending other Kingdom Halls I continued to experience these similar types of opportunities.

Chapter 8
Charitable Giving

Because of the scripture at ***John 13:35***, which states *"By this all will know that you are my disciples, if you have love among yourselves"*, Jehovah's Witnesses make sure to take care of their own. They do this in many ways, and in my experience, they were always sincere about it – it didn't seem to be a matter of mere duty.

My earliest memory was in 1972, when I was only four years old: The Chemung River overflowed and catastrophically flooded Elmira. One of the five bridges was washed away, and homes and businesses were utterly destroyed. Fortunately, we lived on the other end of town where the flood waters didn't reach, so we were safe. However, many of the Jehovah's Witnesses in our congregation were among the many victims of the flood. Donations from surrounding Kingdom Halls came pouring in after the waters receded: Clothing, toys, blankets, appliances, household items, *tons* of donations from Jehovah's Witnesses in the region! Our Kingdom Hall was the holding place for all these items, and the members of our congregation who were flood victims came and gathered whatever donations they could use. After all the victims were finished sorting through everything, the remainder of the congregation's members could sort through and take any of the leftovers they wished. I was only four years old at the time, but I clearly remember being in the Kingdom Hall basement with my mother, sorting through toys and clothing.

In fact, during many disasters, Jehovah's Witnesses immediately begin organizing help for members who need help – it's an automatic response. Usually, after fellow members are served they go on to serve the non-members in the disaster area, if there is anything left to give.

Beyond disasters, they also help members who come upon individual crises. I remember one year I had a high risk pregnancy and was ordered to bed rest until further notice. My husband (who has never been a Jehovah's Witness) was burdened with taking care of me, our two young children, the housework, appointments, and whatever else life threw his way. My husband rose to the challenge: The day I was ordered to bed rest my husband brought our bed out into the living room so I wouldn't have to feel so detached from the family. During the six weeks I was on bed rest he made our meals, did all the cleaning, taught the kids how to call 911 in case he wasn't home if I had an emergency, did all the errands and whatever else needed to be done. Our kids were not yet school aged at the time, but they helped with the housework in a limited way. After a few day, the members of my congregation got together and planned some help for my husband: Each night one of the families would cook a supper for us and drop it off. We'd get some *really* good meals, such as roast chicken with seasoned rice and tossed salad – these families were good cooks! They did this all the way up until I lost the pregnancy. I often prayed that God would bless those generous families!

A few years later, just a few months after we moved out of the area, we got into a major car accident. My husband and our kids were hospitalized. I was the only one able to be released to home, though I had three broken ribs. My new congregation helped in so many ways: The kids were recovering in a children's hospital in a different county, and the members took turns giving me daily transportation to go see them (since my car was destroyed in the accident). They also took me on shopping errands and cleaned our apartment from top to bottom. My husband was released from the hospital before the kids were, so then the members of my congregation began cooking up meals for us and sending them over – they were so generous with the meals that we had to request that nobody send food on Fridays, which we reserved as "left over" nights!

And it wasn't just my own experience; I often saw members of the congregation rally together to help their own, no matter which congregation I went to. Indeed, the Jehovah's Witnesses do take care of their own whether it be a natural disaster, an accident, or a personal crisis – but only to the extent that no one is financially burdened over it.

Occasionally they may help a stranger who's car is broken down on the highway, or help a neighbor in need, but for the most part, beyond helping their own members their charitable acts do not go much further – unless you count their door-to-door ministry as a charitable act (as some do).

Donations to humanitarian charitable organizations is usually discouraged. Their view is that many charities use so much of the donations for their overhead costs, that it almost defeats the purpose of the charity. On top of that, it is also their view that many of the charitable organizations serve "unbiblical purposes"; something a Jehovah's Witness does not want to contribute towards. For example, the Red Cross is a great help in disasters, but they also hold blood drives – since Jehovah's Witnesses believe blood transfusions are unbiblical, they do not wish to donate to the Red Cross. Jehovah's Witnesses also do not donate money to needy children through UNICEF because it originates from the United Nations, an organization that they believe is unbiblical. They also refrain from donating to the Boy Scouts or Girl Scouts charity drives since those were considered to be nationalistic / patriotic groups, another thing to be avoided. They are also wary of donating to *any* organization that has a religious backing, such as The Salvation Army or Catholic Charities, since they don't want to inadvertently support the churches, as Jehovah's Witnesses view all churches as false, satanic religion. Therefore, if a Boy Scouts group is holding a food drive for a local food pantry charity, a Jehovah's Witness is not to donate even a single can of vegetables. If a Wesleyan church is holding a clothing drive for their charity clothes closet, a Jehovah's Witness is not to give so much as a single sock. Salvation Army bell ringers at Christmas? Nope, not a penny. So basically, it means exactly this: There are over 7 million Jehovah's Witnesses in the world, and not one of them will contribute to a blood bank, church based food pantry, world hunger program, sponsor a child overseas, support a church based homeless shelter, give donations to a church clothing program, or any other charitable cause that is run by a religion, patriotic organization, or other "unbiblical" organization. Sadly, this cuts out nearly all humanitarian projects that exist. Just *think* of all the added good there would be if those 7 million members would open up their hearts and give donations to these humanitarian projects!

The real shame of the matter is that, although the Jehovah's Witnesses will not donate to these charities, they have no problem with using these very same charities if they absolutely need them. If a member's home catches fire, it would be okay to use the Red Cross to obtain a motel room for the night. If a member has a bad financial situation, it would be okay to go to Catholic Charities to help pay for your medicinal prescriptions. In the Jehovah's Witness world, the congregation is not expected to be burdened with helping a member financially; it is expected that the member's own family help with what they can, and then use the community charity organizations or social services to cover the rest of the member's needs. So basically, it boils down to this: The Jehovah's Witnesses has no formal charity organization for its own members, restricts members from donating to most humanitarian charities, and yet allows those members to take what they need from those same charities in times of crisis. It's a very one-sided deal.

Even during my believing days, this one-sided view towards charity bothered me. I didn't understand how donating canned food to church food pantries was supporting a church – it wasn't as though the church could use the food for currency! And I didn't understand why we couldn't donate used clothing to the church clothing drives either, for the same reason. Doesn't the bible say to feed your enemies? (***Romans 12:20***) And, if we are to give charity to our known enemies, shouldn't we also be giving charity to strangers too? (***Proverbs 21:13***). Churches, the Boy Scouts, and the Red Cross don't get any benefit from these donations – only the poor and needy do – isn't that what unconditional love is supposed to be about? Of course, the Jehovah's Witnesses claim that they *do* perform a great charitable work by doing the door-to-door preaching – after all, they are saving lives. Although I *did* believe they were saving lives at the time, I didn't see how that should be a *complete* substitute for a needy person's immediate needs; children still needed to eat, babies still needed to be clothed, and homeless people still needed to be sheltered. But again, it was something I didn't understand, and I was to "Wait on Jehovah" and be obedient to The Organization, for they knew better than I.

After I left the Jehovah's Witnesses and began attending local church services, I clearly saw the stark contrast between Jehovah's Witness charity vs. Church charity: Unlike the Jehovah's Witnesses, many churches hold monthly food collections for the local food pantries, hold fund raisers for other charities, blood drives for accident victims, and so on. I've seen churches make holiday food baskets for the poor, and cloth bandages to be sent to field hospitals in third world countries. Compassion moves them to collect coins to support orphanages in eastern Europe and send money specifically for victims in disaster areas. I've seen churches send mission groups to help other churches in foreign countries, send Christmas stocking filled with goodies to ghetto kids in New York City, assemble hygiene kits for people suffering through local catastrophes, and set aside money to help congregation members who have fallen on hard financial times. I never saw anything like that in the Jehovah's Witness world! I loved seeing these acts of generosity being carried out by the churches – it felt *so* right to do these kinds of things! I couldn't see how these acts of love could possibly be wrong – how is unconditional love *ever* wrong? Even the children in the churches are encouraged to be involved in charitable giving, it's considered to be an essential part of living in Christ!

It became clear to me that if every church in the world followed the Jehovah's Witnesses' example, there would be a catastrophic reduction of help for the poor on a global scale! Yes, it's a sobering thought, and I praise God that churches do not practice such severe restrictions in charity.

Chapter 9
Denominational Unity

In the Jehovah's Witness world, "UNITY" is their main goal, and unity means to have the same doctrine and the same mind throughout the brotherhood, and to avoid all outside influences as much as possible. I know I've stated this before, but it's important to understand the Jehovah's Witness mindset: The Organization is directed by Jehovah's Holy Spirit and is Jehovah's visible channel of communication to mankind. Following the Organization's directions is the same as following Jehovah's Commands.

Because they regard The Organization so highly, unity is strictly expected. It is believed that allowing members to deviate from the unity in any way will eventually cause demoralization of the congregation, therefore a member must be "sheep-like" and follow every directive that comes from The Organization. Those who continually resist this unity risk receiving congregational discipline (described in chapter 11). All members are to act in complete agreement as to doctrine and behavior. There is no room for personal opinion unless the Watchtower Society publishes that something can be a matter of personal opinion, a.k.a a "conscience matter". In many ways this can be a good thing, but in other ways this can be unnecessarily restrictive.

In matters of doctrine, Jehovah's Witnesses are to believe only what The Organization publishes through the Watchtower Society; no more, and no less. If The Society publishes a change in doctrine, you were expected to go along with the change. There is no room for openly expressing an opposing personal opinion or alternate understanding of something. This is the reason why a baptismal candidate must go through a long battery of doctrinal questions to answer correctly before being allowed to get baptized. If the baptismal candidate is unable to answer the questions within the confines of The

Organization's doctrine, the candidate will not be allowed baptism at that time. A baptized member must be in complete unity (conformity) with the rest of the brotherhood, therefore the ability to correctly answer the baptismal questions is paramount. Each and every Jehovah's Witness everywhere in the world believes and teaches the same thing.

To openly disagree with the publications, or to willfully teach something different, is considered to be apostasy, and you risk losing your membership as a Jehovah's Witness. One should keep one's disagreements to oneself and wait on Jehovah for a more clear understanding. Period.

Because this unity is an all or nothing deal, this results in many restrictions on a member's life. For example, in the name of unity, no Jehovah's Witness will give or take a blood donation, eat birthday cake, participate in politics or patriotic activities, or visit churches. They will use only the New World Translation Bible in their worship and refuse to read any religious literature from other denominations. All members are to dress modestly, and males are to be clean shaven (mustaches are okay) and keep their hair short. They won't participate in after-school activities, school clubs, or high school pep rallies. They won't listen to heavy metal or hard rock music – not even Christian versions. Dating is only for those who are seeking a spouse, and one should only date within the Jehovah's Witnesses, and with a chaperone (I managed to get my non-Jehovah's Witness husband during a period when I was disfellowshipped – which is explained in Chapter 11). A member is not to become affiliated with social clubs or other "worldly" organizations. Women don't receive positions of congregational responsibility, and families can't attend holiday events. You are expected to schedule your employment and recreational activities around the weekly Bible meetings, and your yearly vacation is spent attending a District Convention. You can't join the military, enroll your child into Boy Scouts or Girl Scouts, buy Girl Scout cookies, or let your children participate in school athletics or academic clubs. Your cannot go to fellowshipping groups in other churches or listen to a Christian radio station or television program. You must avoid your employer's holiday parties and turn down invitations from non-Jehovah's Witnesses. You cannot throw rice at a weddings, and there are no family gatherings for Thanksgiving or Christmas. You are not to display national flags on your lawn, and you are to keep your socialization limited to fellow Jehovah's Witnesses.

It goes on and on.

Although this is a very buttoned-down denomination, this strict unity creates a sense of camaraderie among the brotherhood, even among members who haven't previously met. I remember when our sons were in Golisano's Children's Hospital in Rochester, New York due to our car accident, and I went to visit them the first time. The receptionist on my sons' unit approached me and asked if I were the mother and if I were a Jehovah's Witness (she saw the information on my sons). When I answered in the affirmative she smiled and told me she was a Jehovah's Witness too, and that if I needed anyone to talk to she'd be there. I can't tell you what a comfort that was! My children were facing the dilemmas of life and death, possible forced blood transfusions, and everyone in the hospital was pressuring me. My husband was hospitalized elsewhere, so I didn't even have him around to lean on. And here was a fellow sister that I'd never met before, offering me her company if I ever felt over-my-head. Even now, with my eyes wide opened as to how false the Jehovah's Witness doctrines are, I still appreciated how she offered to be there for me. Being a momma with two sons in the ICU, I needed that!

On the down side though, this strict unity can be mentally crippling. For example, the study literature for the meetings became an exercise in complete and utter boredom most of the time: All members would be studying the same literature during the same weeks, which wasn't so bad in itself. The problem was the tedious format: Read a paragraph. Answer the corresponding question. Read another paragraph. Answer another question. This would occur with the Watchtower Study, the Book Study, and the Kingdom Ministry Sheets each week. It was the format directed by the Organization, therefore it was the format we faithfully stuck to in the spirit of unity. What made it so bad was that the answers had to come straight from the words in the paragraphs; there was very little room to add outside information to the answer. Here's a real life example from a past issue of the Watchtower magazine:

(*The Watchtower*, *December 15th, 2005 study article title, theme text, first paragraph, corresponding questions*)

Whom Do You Obey – God or Man?

"We must obey God as ruler rather than men" – ACTS 5:29

The judges of the Jewish supreme court must have been furious. The prisoners were missing. They were the apostles of Jesus Christ, a man the high court had condemned to death a few weeks earlier. Now the court was ready to deal with his closest followers. But when the guards went to fetch them, they discovered that their cells were empty, although the doors had been locked. The guards soon learned that the apostles were at the temple in Jerusalem, fearlessly teaching the people about Jesus Christ – the very activity for which they had been arrested! The guards went straightaway to the temple, took the apostles back into custody, and brought them to court. – Acts 5:17-27

Questions:

a)What is the theme text for this study?
b) Why were the apostles taken into custody?

This is a true, representative sample of a normal Jehovah's Witness study, whether it be the Sunday Watchtower study, the Tuesday book study, or material for the Thursday Kingdom Ministry School study. Questions were so rote from the paragraphs that no real thinking was involved. Since you are required to accept all the information presented, and stick tight to the reading, there was no opportunity to debate a viewpoint or a doctrinal stand; there was no brain exercise in any of these studies – just simple parroting of the published material. For a paragraph as simple as the above mentioned sample, I would have *loved* to discuss how the apostles must have reacted or felt in this biblical passage. I even would have loved to discuss the viewpoint of the guards for that matter! All I wanted was some mental stimulation to go with the reading, but that was not the way that The Organization directed it to be. For years I kept telling myself that it was necessary to have these studies so simple due to the presence of members who have less intelligence (those who were very young, or those with severe mental retardation, for example), or for those who are new to the Jehovah's Witness faith. I kept in mind that we were all supposed to display unity, which would include ensuring all members could understand the material being studied all at the same time. And yet, I still had the hardest time sitting through each study plodding through the simplicity. But I suppose you didn't really have to think; after all, The Organization did all the thinking for you.

Another mental hardship was the acceptance of doctrine you simply didn't understand. For years I didn't understand how they came to the doctrine of 1914 and Christ's presence. Their explanations of biblical prophecy that they attached to this doctrine was confusing, and whenever it came up in the study material I finally gave up and simply took their word for it. I couldn't question the teaching because that was not acceptable; instead I was to "wait on Jehovah" for understanding, yet again. At the time, I still believed that they were Jehovah's Channel of communication, and so they *must* know what they're talking about, even if I didn't understand it.

It's harder than you'd think to carry around doctrines that you don't understand.

Another hardship that came with this demand for unity was that you had to accept a doctrine that you understood *but* didn't agree with. If you happened to have a different view of a teaching than what The Watchtower Society was publishing, you had to shut up and put up. I remember when I was much younger and one member, Norma, had been abandoned by her husband – he actually had left her for another man. At that time, although homosexuality was considered wrong, it wasn't considered to be an adulterous act on his part. Since Jehovah's Witnesses could only divorce on the grounds of adultery, this poor woman had to wait for several years before The Organization changed their doctrine, which finally allowed her to divorce and remarry. It didn't matter if anyone else realized that the homosexual affair was adulterous, it only mattered whether The Organization recognized it as such.

This strict code of unity also affects the membership in other, less prominent ways. For example, in order to remain in unity with the brotherhood, you must make it to all the meetings every week. If you start missing meetings on a regular basis, the Elders will organize a "Shepherding Call". This is when they arrange to meet with you at your home, at which time they speak with you about your situation: Is there something they can help you with so you can attend more meetings? How is your Bible study schedule? And whatever other questions and solutions they may deem appropriate to your situation. Aside from illness or an unexpected circumstance, it is expected that you will happily attend each meeting every week.

As part of the unity, the Elders and Ministerial Servants would also tally how many members were in attendance at each meeting. I was never sure about why that was necessary, but since the tally was ordered by the powers-that-be in Bethel, it was done without question.

If you have a job that interferes with meeting times, you are expected to do your best to re-arrange your work hours in order to accommodate the meetings. If that isn't possible, you are expected to find another job that *will* accommodate your meeting schedule. In many cases, this means that members end up becoming self-employed: Performing yard work, housecleaning, home based businesses, etc. If you are a new "study" seeking to become a member, and your job involves something outside of the Society's parameters for morality, you must quit that job. Jobs that fall under this would include working for a tobacco company, certain positions at casinos, bar tending, working birthday parties as a clown, etc. I particularly remember one man, Dane, who was newly studying with a member in our congregation. Dane had been unemployed for a while and finally landed a job working at a local tobacco company. He was so thrilled to finally have a job, but then the Elders hit him with the hammer: His work was unbiblical, and so he had to quit that job and find something else. He was given a certain amount of time to do this – it was viewed as a test of his loyalty. He did quit the job, and fortunately didn't take long to find another. However, it would have saved him a lot of trouble if he had been told beforehand that there were restrictions on what kind of job he could accept!

When I was growing up, all college education was discouraged as they taught it was better to spend one's time out in Service instead. Fortunately, that teaching has relaxed over the years; but even so, higher education is carefully scrutinized. According to a 2008 Jehovah's Witness symposium, in the talk titled *"Stand Firm Against the Devil's Crafty Acts in the Field of Education"*, orator Neil Ryan stated that, according to the October 1, 2005 *The Watchtower*, "higher education" is defined as a four-year college or university. His talk continued on to explain how, according to Isaiah 54:13 that children should be taught by Jehovah, not by worldly institutions, discouraging young Jehovah's Witnesses from pursuing a four-year degree.

In the spirit of unity, putting the preaching work on the back burner in deference to higher education is simply not an option for someone who wanted to remain in good standing in the congregation.

This situation happened in 2009 with my brother, Forrest. He had become certified as a Nursing Assistant and was doing really well at the job. Soon he decided he wanted to go further with his education to become a Licensed Practical Nurse. He continued working as a Nursing Assistant, started college classes for nursing, and tried to keep up with all the spiritual duties associated with being a Jehovah's Witness. Although he was single and had no children, the daily load was too much. He felt his Field Service time was becoming lost in the shuffle, and so he eventually quit his nursing classes. I thought it was a crying shame because he only needed to take one year of classes, and he would have made a great nurse and had a good, solid career. But the pressure was on for him to keep his Service hours up, and so he made his choice.

Another part of unity includes the avoidance of associating with non-believers in a recreational manner. This means it is not proper to go out for drinks after work with your co-workers. It is not acceptable to attend your company's summer picnic. All non-believers are considered to be "worldly" and can't be expected to have high enough moral standards; thus a Jehovah's Witness child would be discouraged from playing with non-Jehovah's Witness children.

In the spirit of unity, Jehovah's Witness adults are also discouraged from seeking out non-believing friends. Sure, you are to be courteous to your neighbors and co-workers, but you are not encouraged to cultivate friendships with them (unless, of course, they show interest in your Jehovah's Witness faith). This means you are discouraged from inviting them to your back-yard barbecue, going out for a few drinks with them, accompanying them to a sports event, or any other recreational thing.

Related to the ideal of unity is the concept of bringing honor and glory to Jehovah's name. In their view, this means being *very* concerned about one's outward appearance in the public eye. This is why male members should be beardless and sport close cropped hair cuts, and all members should show up at weekly meetings wearing semi-formal clothing. The Organization is so concerned about the membership's appearance in public that they even went so far as to give these instructions regarding the Assemblies:

> *"Should we manifest a dignified appearance only when attending the program? Remember that many will observe us wearing our convention badges while in the convention city. Our appearance should make us stand out from the general public. Therefore, even during leisure time, such as when going out to eat after the program, we should dress as befits ministers who are in the city for the purpose of attending a Christian convention and should not wear such clothing as jeans, shorts, or T-shirts. What a witness this will give to the community! Jehovah is pleased when our appearance bespeaks our role as ministers."*
>
> ***Our Kingdom Ministry**, April 2007, "Follow The Christ By Manifesting Dignity", par. 5*

In other words, after a long day of sitting through an assembly program, if you want to go sightseeing afterwards they want you to do so in your suit coats and dresses for the sole purpose of standing out from the general public! Incredibly, they don't see this as being in complete contrast with what the Bible says:

> *"And do not let your adornment be that of the external braiding of the hair, and of the putting on of gold ornaments, or the wearing of outer garments, but let it be the secret person of the heart in the incorruptible apparel of the quiet and mild spirit, which is of great value in the eyes of God."*
> ***1 Peter 3:3-4***

The other half of their concept of bringing honor and glory to Jehovah is to absolutely avoid all "appearances of evil".

The "appearance of evil" covers a lot of ground: Do not spend unaccountable time alone with an unrelated member of the opposite sex, or with a known homosexual. Do not go into a bar (even if you simply have to use its restroom), and be sure to cross the street rather than be seen walking past an adult entertainment venue. Don't buy a pack of cigarettes for your non-Witness relative, don't eat the holiday treats at the office, and don't give your next door neighbor a ride to his or her church. Don't attend an R-rated movie, don't cohabit platonically with an unrelated member of the opposite gender, don't listen to hip-hop music, don't pray in public with non-believers, and don't laugh at an inappropriate joke – even if it *is* funny. As a good Jehovah's Witness, you were not to give anyone an occasion to speak abusively of your faith or question your solidarity of faith, for that was bringing reproach upon Jehovah. I remember an incident when a married Elder took a long road trip a few states away with a female member of the congregation who was not his wife. The female needed the transportation for an urgent matter. However, even though it was a completely innocent matter, this was considered to be "unaccountable time" because there wasn't a third person in the car to accompany them. As a result, the pair were judicially reproved for the incident. (explained in chapter 11).

Therefore, a good Jehovah's Witness will abide by all the rules and regulations imposed, even if there is no biblical requirement to do so. One's complete obedience to Jehovah's Organization on earth is viewed as a display of one's complete obedience to Jehovah God. Since the men in The Governing Body are directed by Jehovah's Holy Spirit, then everything that comes from them must have a good reason for it. This means that, aside from the other displays of unity already listed in this chapter, congregations are required to: Count the members who are present at each meeting, count the number of attendees that come to the yearly Memorial, count the number of partakers at the Memorial, count the number of hours members spend out in Service, count the number of items the Publishers place when out in Service, count the number of those who get baptized each year, avoid watching holiday television specials, disallow beards and long hair on males (hair that reaches past the collar), completely shun ex-Jehovah's Witnesses, and associate only with other Jehovah's Witnesses.

The entire scope of "unity" was a little confusing for me growing up though, and I'll tell you why: Although my parents were very strong believers, they allowed us a little wiggle room from these regulations in some ways, while at the same times they were strictly adherent to the regulations in other ways. In other words, they let us play outside with the neighborhood kids, watch the Charlie Brown holiday specials, stay up late on New Year's Eve to watch the ball drop in Times Square, and let Amelia go on a few dates with a "worldly" boy in high school. On the other hand, they would tell us how ugly the neighborhood Christmas lights were every year, refuse to let my brother Shane read ninja magazines, and ensure we had all our studies and devotionals finished every day of every week. Our family bookshelf was confusing too, for not only did it hold Watchtower literature, but it also had a Dianetics book, a Book of Mormon, and a Catholic Bible . As far as I know, Dad and Mom were never spoken to about these things, but then again I'm not sure how well these things were known by our Elders either.

I'm sure my parents weren't intending to have double standards, I assume their laxness had something to do with the fact that they weren't born and raised into the faith. Regardless, even with the "relaxed" rules at home, there were still boundaries in place: We could play with the neighborhood kids, but only in the yards (no overnights, no dinners, etc). We could watch the ball drop in Times Square, but we couldn't have a party to go along with it. The non-Jehovah's Witness religious books on the shelf were for reference purposes only and not something to be actually studied. We could watch the Charlie Brown Christmas special, but not the "Rudolph the Red Nose Reindeer" cartoon movie. Since I had grown up with these double standards I didn't think much about them; I just went along with whatever Dad and Mom decided.

In spite of our parents relaxing of some of the rules, we still considered ourselves to be a devout Jehovah's Witness family. In the spirit of unity, we faithfully attended all the meetings, all the Assemblies, and studied all the materials each week. We avoided holiday and birthday events, participated in the

Theocratic Ministry School on a regular basis, and did our door-to-door ministry as directed. We helped clean the Kingdom Hall a couple of times each year, volunteered to help out at Assemblies, and participated in congregational events. Although we may not have been a perfect Jehovah's Witness family, we did highly value the "glue" of unity in our membership.

Chapter 10
Holidays and Birthdays

It is a well-known fact that Jehovah's Witnesses do not celebrate any holidays or birthdays throughout the year. This is because Jehovah's Witnesses are very concerned with keeping their worship spotless from all forms of false worship, as well as keeping themselves separate from the world. Therefore, Jehovah's Witnesses have nothing to do with Christmas, Easter, Halloween, Patriotic Events, Thanksgiving, Religious Holidays, National Holidays, or days that commemorate people such as birthdays, Mother's Day and Saint Patrick's Day.

Because my siblings and I attended a public Elementary school, we often had to deal with classroom holiday events. Our parents would speak to our teachers at the beginning of the school year to arrange for us to go to the school library during these classroom events. The teachers were always accommodating, and the librarian was a lovely lady that welcomed us every time. Due to the frequency of classmates' birthdays and the holidays, we saw the school library *a lot*. It didn't bother me though because the library had a large selection of reading materials, as well as several mini film projectors with which we could watch short films. Not only that, but it also afforded us an opportunity to finish our homework, freeing up our time later. Once in a while, the school would skip the education for the afternoon classes and hold big holiday parties instead. In cases like this, we could choose between staying in the library the whole afternoon or just going home early.

Because the Jehovah's Witnesses always had other recreational events planned throughout the year I didn't feel too much like I was missing out on these things. Of course, I was still always *curious* about these holidays and birthdays, and wondered what it was like to celebrate them, especially when I'd see the neighborhood holiday decorations when we traveled back and forth to our Bible meetings. But, instead of celebrating the holidays, we'd spend our time explaining to others why we didn't celebrate.

When we were kids we'd take turns answering the door on Halloween, telling the trick-or-treaters that we didn't celebrate Halloween. I remember one year I asked my parents about handing out our religious tracts to the trick-or-treaters, but that was forbidden; any kind of giving of anything to the kids was considered as being a celebration of Halloween. I didn't understand it, as I was thinking it was a good way to "witness" to the kids. But, again, who was I to question the Organization's direction?

In my adult life I had to navigate the holidays at my places of employment. If I worked in a department store I politely excused myself from setting up holiday displays. I politely declined to take part in holiday office parties. Sometimes, though, I could skirt around the issue. For example, one year I was working at a fabric store and the boss wanted us to wear aprons with a Christmas themed iron-on decoration. I did my own iron-on that was still winter themed, but without the Christmas details. The customers didn't really notice my decorations as being   different so my boss was happy with it and all was fine.

Another thing I had to navigate was my husband. He had never been a Jehovah's Witness, and wasn't planning to become one, so the holidays presented a few challenges, but we managed to work it out. We agreed that we wouldn't decorate the home for any of the holidays, and in return I wouldn't complain if he took the kids to attend his family's holiday get-togethers and birthday events. Since he was their father and the head of the household, I didn't feel wrong for letting him do so. Instead, I took these opportunities as teaching moments for the kids, discussing the pros and cons of holidays and birthdays and what it meant for us as Jehovah's Witnesses. For Thanksgiving, we'd have our turkey feast on a day *near* Thanksgiving, but not actually on Thanksgiving day.

I also followed my parents' example when we were growing up and bought Easter and Valentine's candies *after* the holidays instead of for the holidays.

Of course, these arrangements between us changed immediately after I left the Jehovah's Witnesses. Although I was still trying to figure out my stand on the holidays at that point, I wasn't going to worry about all the details anymore. The first holiday to tackle was Thanksgiving because I was disfellowshipped (excommunicated) from the congregation around Thanksgiving time that year. My whole life growing up as a Jehovah's Witness, I was told that we didn't celebrate Thanksgiving because it was nationalistic, and that we should be giving thanks *every day*, not just once per year. Even when I was a devout Jehovah's Witness I never did see why it was viewed as nationalistic; it's not like there were patriotic decorations or songs attached to the holiday. And I never understood why we couldn't set aside a particular day for thanks even when we are thankful all the other days. But since the Organization said so, I went along with it for the sake of unity. NOW, though, I had broken out of that mindset, and since I couldn't find anything objectionable about the holiday, I decided that celebrating it on the actual day was no crime. Therefore, that very year, we had our first family Thanksgiving feast.

It went mostly well – only my fourteen year old son had an issue with it. You see, he was still trying to figure out his own faith and was continuing to attend the meetings at the Kingdom Hall in the meantime. Since Thanksgiving is always on a Thursday, and Bible meetings were always on a Thursday as well, he was upset that the members coming to pick him up would see the Thanksgiving celebration going on. I reminded him that they wouldn't fault him for something that *I* was doing, and that this was a great opportunity for him to ask them the Jehovah's Witness reasons for shunning the holiday. I figured that if he got the same weak reasons that I grew up with, it would help him feel less bad about celebrating it. My son's dilemma of faith didn't last longer than a few months, though and by the following year he had stopped attending the Kingdom Hall as well, and was open to celebrating holidays and birthdays.

With Thanksgiving out of the way, my husband went right out and bought our first artificial Christmas Tree. He bought a six foot tree and then took the kids to the store to choose decorations and lights and things. Meanwhile, I was still in the midst of trying to figure myself out, so I didn't participate in any of it. I grew up with the Jehovah's Witness belief that most of the Christmas traditions stemmed from paganism, which is why they always shunned the holiday. Now, I had to figure out how much did I really agree with that point of view. Was I really honoring false gods by participating? Or was it no longer an issue anymore? Although I wasn't decided, I did participate in the buying of family gifts though, and by the time Christmas rolled around our tree was filled with gifts underneath.

It actually took me a couple of Christmases to finally figure out where I stood on the matter. I had finally decided that, since even the *angels* celebrated Christ's birth (Luke 2:9-14), then how could it be wrong for *people* to celebrate it as well? The first coming of our Saviour was one of the greatest things that ever happened to mankind – how could it *possibly* be wrong to celebrate *that*! I still had my hang-ups regarding the pagan stuff though, so I decided I'd simply discard all the pagan traditions and just keep the things that put the focus on Christ. I knew my husband wanted to keep the Christmas tree though, so I started buying decorations that were more Christ centered. I also took to reading Christmas related bible passages to the children and watching Christ-centered Christmas DVD's. I also didn't make an issue of it if they wanted to watch Santa Claus movies and such – they all knew that Santa was mere fantasy so I viewed it as I would if they watched any other fictional children's movie.

I went through a similar thing with Easter: As I was still figuring out Christmas, I was also trying to figure out Easter (since both holidays are related). Again, I concluded that the death of Christ was among the greatest things that ever happened to mankind. And again, I also concluded that discarding the pagan traditions and simply keeping the Christ-centered traditions was the way to go. Instead of Easter Baskets, I began making Resurrection Baskets: Candy Coins to symbolize the money paid to Judas, chocolate crosses, white chocolate lambs, etc. , and the kids were happy with it.

Mother's Day and Father's Day gave me no issues. Since scripture says we must honor our parents (*Exodus 20:12, Ephesians 6:2*), it made sense that these days should be commemorated. And, since I no longer had the boys in Bethel telling me what a bad bad thing it was to give such honor to someone, I gladly embraced these opportunities for honor. Of course, I wasn't able to honor my *own* parents because they would be offended by the gesture since they remained as Jehovah's Witnesses, but I did begin to honor my in-laws and my husband on these days.

As for the patriotic events, I learned to navigate that one pretty carefully. I still don't like the idea of pledging my allegiance to anyone or anything other than God, but I *do* totally appreciate living in a free country with freedom of choice. I totally appreciate the men and women who fought for those freedoms, and I totally appreciate that some of them paid for these freedoms with their dear lives. I still believe in giving due honor to my country's leaders, I still believe in paying my taxes, and I still give due respect to the politicians whom I didn't vote for. I still believe that God places the politicians in their positions (*Romans 13:1-7*), thus I don't believe in trying to work against the system. So I finally came to the conclusion that I would participate in the celebration of our freedom and the blessings that come with it, though I would continue to refrain from pledging my allegiance to anyone but God. So we started taking the kids to watch Fourth-Of-July fireworks, Memorial Day parades, and Patriot Day parades.

Halloween was another one that I had to figure out. By the time I was disfellowshipped, our two older kids had outgrown the age of trick-or-treating; however, our youngest one was plenty young enough to have a few years left for it. Since I was on the fence about it, I didn't make an issue out of it when my husband decided to start taking him out trick-or-treating. Our son did it for a couple of years, but he then decided on his own that he would rather *give* the candy rather than take it. So he began carving a pumpkin with Christian symbols, put a light in it and sit outside on the porch with it and give out candy. At the end of the night there was always plenty of candy left over for him to keep, so he didn't miss out on the goodies. Eventually, I came to a conclusion about Halloween: We should take the night that celebrates monsters and shine the light of Jesus in it. Doing this was easy: We began putting the candies in little snack baggies along with child-oriented Christian comic tracts in each of the baggies. Although our youngest is now older, he continues to enjoy giving out the double-treat bags to the kids.

Birthdays weren't too foreign to my kids because my in-laws sometimes had birthday parties for them from time to time. Now, the Jehovah's Witness view is that Birthdays are bad because the only two birthday parties mentioned in the bible each involved a beheading, on top of the idea that birthday parties involve giving too much honor to a person. Again, even when I was a devout Jehovah's Witness, I thought this was weak reasoning: If we couldn't have birthday parties due to two ancient murders, why can we have baby showers, after all, isn't a baby shower a type of birthday party? But of course, questioning this was resisting the unity, so I kept it to myself. But now that I was no longer a Jehovah's Witness, the Society no longer had any power over me, and I was free to celebrate the lives of my children! It took me a couple of tries to get the birthday "thing" right (when to send out invitations, what kinds of entertainment to provide), but with my husband's guidance I managed to get the knack of it.

Over time I managed to successfully shed my major hang-ups, and I learned to enjoy the special days throughout the year. Although I don't regret having missed out on these things when I was growing up, I'm still glad that I'm free to celebrate them now.

Chapter 11
Disciplining Procedures

Disciplining a wayward member of a Jehovah's Witness congregation was a very formal matter, and the Elders were the ones who always handled these situations. Elders are given a special handbook published by the Watchtower Society titled *"Pay Attention To Yourselves and to All the Flock"* that instructs them on how to handle various matters in the congregation, including matters of discipline, according to the Society's direction. Each Elder receives a copy of the book, and returns the book if he relinquishes his position as an Elder.

The method of discipline depended upon how many people witnessed the offense, the offense committed, and the attitude of the wayward member. There were three primary methods of discipline:

1. **Judicial Reproof:** If a member has committed a sin and is repentant, he or she would be given what is called "Judicial Reproof". This is done when there is at least two witnesses to the sin, or a confession of the sin. In most cases, this reproof is performed privately. In more extreme cases, such as when many members of the congregation already know about the sin, it may be deemed necessary to publicly announce the reproof at one of the meetings -- though the actual sin itself is not announced. When a member has been reproved, he or she also loses certain privileges within the congregation. For reproved Elders, Ministerial Servants, and Pioneers, this would mean losing their respective positions. For regular members, this would mean being restricted from answering study questions, praying in a group, and loss of special service privileges, such as taking part

in an assembly drama or a skit on the Kingdom Hall stage.

2. **Disfellowshipping:** If you were a baptized member who was willfully committing sin, you risked being disfellowshipped. To be disfellowshipped means that you are no longer considered to be one of Jehovah's Witnesses. However, because you once *were* a baptized member, your disfellowshipping is seen as leaving Jehovah – which is a grave sin. A disfellowshipped member is shunned by the congregation.

3. **Restriction:** If, after you've been disfellowshipped you decide to come back, you first must prove you have ceased your sinful course and that you sincerely want to come back to the flock. Once your sincerity has been established, the Elders will announce that you've been "reinstated" into the congregation. Then, for a short time period after your return, you will have restricted privileges, similar to one who has undergone Judicial Reproof, for a brief period of time.

If any member deviates from the prescribed parameters of unity or is caught in sin, he or she runs the risk of receiving one of the above disciplinary actions. Reproof and restrictions are viewed as a "marking", in reference to *2 Thessalonians 3:14-15*, which states:

> *"But if anyone is not obedient to our word through this letter, keep this one marked, stop associating with him, that he may become ashamed. And yet do not be considering him as an enemy, but continue admonishing him as a brother"*

They explain the actions of reproof and and restrictions as necessary,   claiming that it prevents the spiritually weak members from influencing the stronger members in a bad way. They base this on the scriptural verse at *1 Corinthians 15:33* *"Bad associations spoil useful habits"* .

Although I understood where they're coming from on that, I didn't understand why such discipline should affect one's desire to be a Pioneer, answer questions at the studies, or pray in a group. Shouldn't acts of worship be *encouraged* instead of discouraged in such cases? Isn't taking acts of worship away from a spiritually weak member the same as withholding food from a person with Anorexia Nervosa? It especially puzzled me in cases of disfellowshipped ones who had become newly reinstated – they'd already gone through their punishment, so how was a period of restriction supposed to be a forgiveness? Where was the scriptural precedent with that? Wouldn't involvement in acts of worship be a beneficial thing for them? Again I had to wait on Jehovah's for understanding in these matters, after all, the Organization was being directed by Jehovah, and I wasn't to question them.

When a member was Judicially Reproved, it was generally understood that the member was considered to be bad association; meaning nobody wanted to socialize with him or her in any capacity. Of course, you were allowed to speak to the person and greet them and such, but you certainly didn't want to socialize outside the Kingdom Hall. And *that* was another thing I didn't understand: The Bible says that we are supposed to encourage those who are weak (*Romans 14:1, 15:1-2*), it doesn't anything about giving them the cold shoulder. I mean, I can see the reason behind not spending one-on-one time together, but wouldn't the weak member benefit from *group* fellowship with stronger members? But again, what did I know. I had to go along with it; after all, we all had to display a unified front.

Unity.

I've never been Judicially Reproved, but I've seen it happen to others. The worst part was, the reproof and restrictions could go on for as long as the Elders decided it should. It could be a week, it could be months. It was very subjective. And, since the Elders are not perfect men, sometimes this happens unjustly.

I particularly remember an occasion that happened to my nephew, Grant. He was a young adult at the time, when one of the sisters of the congregation (who was also about his age) falsely accused him of touching her inappropriately. This sister just happened to be the daughter of one of the "anointed ones" in the congregation. There were no witnesses to the accusation, but they took her word for it anyway and Grant was Judicially Reproved and restricted. This was totally against the rules, for there is supposed to be at least *two* witnesses to the offense – and in this case it was just her word against his. Grant was angry and humiliated, but there was nothing he could do about it. Some time later, this sister confessed to one of her friends that she made the whole thing up. The friend told the Elders, and the Elders reversed his restrictions and reproof. *HOWEVER*, not only did nobody apologize to him for the whole episode, but the girl who falsely accused him received absolutely no consequences for the awful trouble she caused him. I can't help but believe that, because she was the daughter of an anointed member, they went light on her. That was just plain wrong. But, of course, who was I to question the Elders.

Disfellowshipping was worse than receiving reproof and restrictions. The point of being disfellowshipped is for the sinner to achieve sadness in a "godly way" in order to draw the sinner to repentance:

> *2 Corinthians 7:10-11* *"For sadness in a godly way makes for repentance to salvation that is not to be regretted...For look! This very thing, your being saddened in a godly way , what a great earnestness it produced in you...clearing of yourselves...righting of the wrong"*

Disfellowshipping, though not a word in the Bible , is based on sins mentioned in various Bible passages. Disfellowshipping offenses could include (among other things):

> *Fornication, greed, idolatry, reviling, drunkenness, extortion,* (*1 Corinthians 5:11-13*), *Adultery, homosexuality, thievery* (*1 Corinthians 6:9-10*), *Apostasy, heresy, blasphemy,* (*Matthew 12:31, 2 Timothy 2:16, Titus 3:10*), *Tobacco use* (*2 Corinthians 7:1*), *Divorce and remarriage, not due to adultery* (*Matthew 19:9*), *Attending a non-Jehovah's Witness worship service* (*2 Corinthians 6:14-17*)

A Disfellowshipping is a severe form of excommunication. A person accused of a disfellowshipping offense is asked to face a Judicial Committee. This is a meeting in which three Elders from the congregation gather privately with the accused member to discuss the situation. If the Elders decide that the accused is guilty of the sin and is unrepentant for the sin, the accused will be disfellowshipped. The disfellowshipped person is no longer considered to be a member of the congregation, but is still allowed to attend Bible meetings. However, this person is not allowed to fellowship to the other members whether inside or outside the Kingdom Hall, answer questions at the congregational studies, attend any Jehovah's Witness recreational activities, or go out in Service. They are restricted as to which congregational literature they can receive, and can't have contact with their own family members in the faith unless they live with him or her, or if it is an emergency. You are taught that anyone who happens to die while in a disfellowshipped state will not be resurrected in the New Order. And, worst of all, it is believed that the prayers of a disfellowshipped person are not heard by Jehovah.

Once a person is disfellowshipped, they must work through a lot of requirements if they wish to be reinstated into the congregation. Reinstatement is based on the biblical passage at **2 Corinthians 2:6-8**:

> *"This rebuke given by the majority is sufficient for such a man., so that, on the contrary now, you should kindly forgive and comfort him that somehow such a man may not be swallowed up by his being overly sad. Therefore I exhort you to confirm your love for him."*

To be reinstated, the ex-member must first give the Elders a letter stating their intent to work towards reinstatement. The Elders arrange to meet with the ex-member to discuss whether the original offense is still an issue, what the ex-member plans for the future, and what the ex-member must do in order to get reinstated. In most cases, the ex-member must begin attending each and every meeting as much as possible, even if that means walking several miles to get there, since congregational members are not allowed to give them rides to the meetings. The ex-member must dress in attire proper for the Kingdom Hall. In cases of the in-home book studies, disfellowshipped ones were to attend the book study gathering at the Kingdom Hall. The person must also forsake all "worldly" association as a display of leaving the world and coming back to Jehovah. The only "worldly" persons allowed would be members of one's own family. The hard part about this is that you still aren't allowed to associate with other Jehovah's Witnesses, yet you still cannot associate with non-Jehovah's Witnesses – meaning you have a time period of seclusion and friendlessness. It can take anywhere from several months to a couple of years of doing all these things before they decide that you've proven yourself worthy and reinstate you.

If a member of your immediate family were disfellowshipped, then you were allowed day-to-day contact if the member lived with you, though you weren't allowed to have spiritual discussions with them. Even though the Bible states that a husband is the spiritual head of his home, (*Ephesians 5:21-24, 6:4*) The Watchtower Society published that disfellowshipped husbands were *not* to conduct a family Bible study, not share their spiritual views of sitting in on the family study, and that the Witness members should say their own silent prayers when the husband leads the family in prayer (*The Watchtower,* September 15, 1981 p. 28, para 12, *Our Kingdom Ministry* August 2002. article "Display Christian Loyalty if a Relative is Disfellowshipped ", paragraph 7). Of course, these rules are completely unbiblical; it's a blatant show of how the Organization is placing themselves above a husband's God-given headship, but at the time I believed they had a better understanding of scripture and so I didn't argue the point.

Although I've never been reproved, I have been disfellowshipped; twice in fact.

The first time I was disfellowshipped was when I was nineteen years old, two years after my baptism. I was living in my own apartment, and had fallen into the wrong crowd. I began smoking cigarettes. My sister, Amelia, turned me in to the Elders for it, though they wouldn't tell me it was her. I knew it was her though, because I never smoked outside my home (because I didn't want to get caught). She and my unbaptized older brother, Quentin, were the only ones in my family that would come visit me. Since Quentin smoked too, I knew it wasn't him. Amelia, on the other hand, had just gotten pregnant by a married man and was in trouble with the congregation. Of course she turned me in. And yes, years later it was confirmed that she was indeed the informant.

I could have fought the disfellowshipping due to the fact that they didn't have two witnesses to my offense, but I decided not to. After all, I *was* smoking, and I knew it was wrong, and that I deserved the consequences. On top of that I was also secretly living with a boyfriend, which was another disfellowshipping offense (though they only got me for the smoking). Soon after my disfellowshipping Amelia was also disfellowshipped for unrepentant fornication – her growing pregnancy being the necessary proof of her actions. Amelia and I saw each other frequently, since we were both disfellowshipped, and quite often we even spent time with Quentin. Since Quentin was never baptized, and he didn't go to the congregational meetings anymore, he just kinda dropped off the "radar", meaning he received no consequences for associating with us.

A few years later, I got serious about quitting the cigarettes, broke up with the boyfriend, and began attending meetings again. I still wholly believed in the Jehovah's Witness doctrine, and I wanted back in. When I started attending, Amelia got interested in being reinstated too, so we often shared a cab to the meetings. By this time she had her three-year-old son, and I had an out-of-wedlock baby, so it took some coordination for the both of us to get to the meetings on time! It took two years for me to get reinstated – *two* years!

What was truly unfair was that Amelia was reinstated a year before I was, and I'll tell you why that was so unfair: The day she was reinstated, she had just had another out-of-wedlock baby by another man, hadn't completely quit smoking, and had another secret boyfriend on top of it. She lived only two miles away from the Kingdom Hall yet Dad and Mom were allowed to give her rides to all the meetings before her reinstatement. Now, the deal with reinstatement is that you have to have already ceased your sins and proven yourself acceptable to the congregation, and yet she didn't have to prove anything: She was pregnant, smoking, fornicating...she didn't even have to find her own way to the meetings, that was taken care of! *MEANWHILE*...I had married my husband (we had been living together for a year prior to our wedding), quit tobacco completely, forsook all my bad associations and was trudging myself to the meetings two miles each way, three times per week, through all kinds of weather. Although I was happy for Amelia, I was angry because I didn't understand why they were being so tough on *me:* It was taking *so* long for my reinstatement, in fact , that towards the end of that two years some of the members of the congregation were starting to offer me rides to meetings when they saw me walking – even they were feeling that it was too long! I finally confronted the elders and asked them exactly what was I doing so wrong that they wouldn't reinstate me. Their reasoning was that in the past year they had rushed a few reinstatements, resulting in those members getting re-disfellowshipped and they didn't want to make that same mistake again. I boldly reminded them that I had been living "clean" and attending the meetings for *two years*. They reinstated me within two weeks; it was the summer of 1993.

By the time I was reinstated, Amelia was re-disfellowshipped, primarily due to her secret boyfriend and her continued smoking.

The second time I was disfellowshipped was in 2004 when I was thirty-six years old. I had begun to openly question many of the doctrines from the Organization, and I wasn't making any friends in the process. The following chapter details the events that led up to this.

Chapter 12
My Awakening

It was a January evening in 2004. I was a content and devoted Jehovah's Witness still in good standing in my congregation. This particular night I happened to be perusing the Internet, as usual. I don't remember now what it was I was looking for, but I sure found something that I *wasn't* looking for: I stumbled upon this rumor that the Watchtower Bible and Tract Society had been a **N**on-**G**overnmental **O**rganization in association with the United Nations for ten years, and that by doing so they had agreed to support the UN! I laughed at the thought: The Watchtower Organization considered the United Nations to be **The Beast** mentioned in the book of Revelation – of course they'd *never* have any association with them! Examples of their view of the UN can be seen in their literature:

> "The United Nations is actually a worldly confederacy against Jehovah God and his dedicated Witnesses on earth." (**The Watchtower**, September 1, 1987, p.20)

> "Human governments have schemed to form the most brazen and defiant conspiracy against divine rule that has ever existed. (Compare Isaiah 8:11-13.) They have done so, not once, but twice, creating first the League of Nations and then the United Nations." (**Awake!** December 8, 1990, p.24)

> What was the "disgusting thing that causes desolation" in the first century, and what is it today? (Matthew 24:15) [gt chapter 111] In 66 c.e it was the Roman armies that surrounded Jerusalem; today it is the United Nations. (**Our Kingdom Ministry**, August 1994 pp.5-6 Theocratic Ministry School Review)

> *Anointed Christians are like alien residents living in tents apart from this system of things. Not even a plague draws near their tent. Whether our hope is heavenly or earthly, we are no part of the world, and we are not infected by such spiritually deadly plagues as its immorality, materialism, false religion, and worship of the "wild beast" and its "image" the United Nations. (**The Watchtower,** November 15, 2001 p.19, paragraph 14)*

However, as I thought about this rumor I decided I'd better prepare a solid answer for it, since I might run into this lie in my door-to-door work. It would be pretty humiliating to come up against this and have no prepared response to defend my faith with! So I began by researching this rumor in order to find it's weaknesses (because every rumor has a weakness). As I researched this rumor online I found that it had been circulating for couple of years, but still I had no hard proof for defense. All I found was the same basic rumor repeated over and over again on different websites. Because I could see that this was apparently a widespread rumor, I was surprised that I hadn't heard it before. However, now that I knew it existed I couldn't let this go on the back burner; I needed to be able to defend The Organization if someone ever confronted me with this. So I tried a different tactic: I contacted the United Nations Department of Public Information and asked them point blank about the rumor.

Yes I did.

I was informed that, indeed, the Watchtower Bible and Tract Society had been an NGO in association with them, starting with their membership being granted in 1992. They had also confirmed that the Society agreed to supporting the work of the United Nations as part of the requirements of being an NGO.

I was stunned – Surely, there must be some kind of mistake!

I took a few minutes to recompose myself, and then the next thing I did was contact the Watchtower headquarters *itself* to get their side of the matter.

Yes I did.

Although the headquarters was a large complex of buildings with a large number of workers, it didn't take long for me to get someone on the line. That was encouraging, for about all of one minute. Since I was an honest and sincere Jehovah's Witness calling the headquarters of honesty and sincerity, I was completely honest in explaining my reason for the call. The receptionist transferred me to another department instead. When that *next* receptionist answered, I explained myself again, after which I was transferred to yet *another* department. When that receptionist answered, I again explained myself, and found myself transferred to *yet another* department.

Apparently I was the hot potato that nobody wanted to hold.

Finally, I was transferred to a phone with a male voice on the line. I don't recall him giving me his name, but I didn't worry about names at this time – I considered this to be the most trusted Organization in the world, names weren't an issue. For the umpteenth time I explained my reason for the call. The man insisted that what the UN told me was not the whole story. He explained that the Watchtower Society had been using the UN library for many years, but in 1991 the rules changed for library use, requiring them to become an NGO in association with the UN in order to be allowed continued access to the library. Therefore, they applied for membership, which was granted in 1992. Then he stated that the requirements for membership had changed some time later – requirements that they couldn't stand by – and therefore they withdrew their membership. I was even referred to a letter that The Watchtower Society circulated in November 2001. I obtained a copy of this letter, which stated:

"*Because of published allegations by opposers that we have secret links with the United Nations, a number of branches have inquired about the matter and we have replied. This circular letter replaces any replies we have given earlier and is sent to all branches. To anyone inquiring within your branch territory you might respond according to what is stated below:*

Our purpose for registering with the Department of Information as a nongovernmental organization (NGO) in 1991 was to have access to research materials available on health, ecological and social problems at the United Nations library facilities. We had been using the library for many years prior to 1991, but in that year it became necessary to register as an NGO to have continued access. Registration papers filed with the United Nations that we have on file contain no statements that conflict with our Christian beliefs. Moreover, NGOs are informed by the United Nations that "association of NGOS with the DPI does not constitute their incorporation into the United Nations system, nor does it entitle associated organizations or their staff to any kind of privileges, immunities, or special status.

Still, the Criteria for Association of NGOs – at least in their latest version – contain language that we cannot subscribe to. When we realized this, we immediately withdrew our registration. We are grateful that this matter was brought to our attention."

So, naturally, my curiosity was piqued and I began looking into what kinds of crazy requirements the UN would have that would cause the Watchtower Society to rescind their membership. I went online to the United Nations official website and searched through their documents. First thing I went after was the rules regarding access to the UN library system. Since the Society claimed in their letter that they were required to be an NGO to continue using the library, I especially looked to see what that was all about. According to the UN, on their "United Nations Depository Library page, it states:

> "*Since 1946, the Dag Hammarskjold Library of the United Nations Secretariat in New York has arranged for the distribution of United Nations documents and publications to users around the world through its depository library system. At present, there are more than 400 depository libraries in over 140 countries maintaining United Nations material from the date of designation as depository to the present. The general public can consult the material free of charge at any depository library."*

Plain as day, the general public has had unfettered access to the UN library materials *since 1946* ; there was absolutely *no* change in this access as the Watchtower Society was claiming! And since there were several of these freely accessible depository libraries right there in New York City where they were located, there was no excuse for anything! The truth screamed at me: Nobody has ever been required to be an NGO in association with the United Nations to access these libraries, *ever!*

I was disgusted to find that the Watchtower Society was blatantly lying about this.

Since the Watchtower Society's letter also alluded to a *"latest version"* of NGO criteria that contained *"language that we cannot subscribe to"*, I also investigated this "latest version" in the UN documents as well. The only version to be found was the *original* that was created in 1968. This is what I found:

> *According to the ECOSOC Resolution 1296, dated May 23 1968, an organization seeking to be an NGO in association with the UN, the following introduction is stated in part:*

> *"Recognizing that arrangements for consultation with non-governmental organizations provide an important means of furthering the purposes and principles of the United Nations"*
> Among the principals listed for NGO association, is listed:
>
> 2. *"The aims and purposes of the organization <u>shall be in conformity with the spirit, purposes and principles of the Charter of the United Nations</u>.*
> 3. *The <u>organization shall undertake to support the work of the United Nations</u> and to promote knowledge of its principles and activities, in accordance with its own aims and purposes and the nature and scope of its competence and activities."*

I was dumbfounded. There had been <u>no</u> changes since it's origination in 1968. This meant that the "*latest version*" that contained "*language*" that they could no longer "*subscribe to*", was the very same original document that was set in 1968 and continues *the same* up to today – that so called "*language*" they could not "*subscribe to*" was already in place the moment they signed up as an NGO!

Next, just to be sure I had the entire picture, I investigated the "*language*" of this criteria, since The Watchtower Society claimed the language contained requirements they could not subscribe to. One of these requirements included being '*in conformity with the spirit, purposes, and principles of the Charter of the United Nations*".

This led me to search out the UN Charter. Now, the Charter does have virtuous motives, such as worldwide peace and such, but it supports this peace through <u>man's</u> efforts, not God. Meanwhile, the Watchtower Society has always taught Jehovah's Witnesses that only Jehovah can bring worldwide peace, and that its an affront to God to try to accomplish it by human means. The UN also supports the use of military force at times, which is something that is against the Watchtower Society's published doctrine of neutrality. The Watchtower Society also teaches the Jehovah's Witness membership to not be a part of the "world", to avoid participating in nationalistic activities, and to avoid politics. Signing up as an NGO in association with the UN meant compromising of all these very doctrines they were teaching us. And, since Jehovah's Witness literature teaches that the UN is a *"worldly confederacy against Jehovah God"*, and is the *"wild beast"* of Revelation, it was completely hypocritical of them to involve themselves into something that is in *conformity with the spirit, purposes, and principles of the Charter of the United Nations*, or to *support the work of the United Nations*!

The Watchtower Society /Organization had clearly been sleeping with the "enemy". I felt cheated on by my own religious leaders. I was beginning to feel sick to my stomach.

On some websites there was talk about The Watchtower Society not realizing the requirements involved, but I knew that couldn't be true. First of all, NGO members were required to reapply for membership annually. This means that they would *have* to know the requirements in order to continue their NGO status for *ten whole years*. If they hadn't completed the necessary requirements in the first place, they would not have been accepted as an NGO year by year. One of the requirements necessary for maintaining NGO status included disseminating information about the UN, publicizing UN events and and activities, and publicizing UN observances. Since they had been an NGO for ten continuous years, they *had* to be submitting these kinds of articles on a regular basis in order to maintain their NGO status! I combed through my Jehovah's Witness literature to see if such articles existed.

Indeed, they did.

Although I didn't have access to *all* the examples of such articles, here are some that I did happen to find that were published   during   their   time   of   membership:

> *Awake!:* September 8, 1991, pp. 3-4, 8-10
> Small series of articles
> *Awake!:* December 8, 1992, p.3 "Resolved to Help

the Children"
The Watchtower: October 1, 1995 pp. 3-4 "Fifty
Years of Frustrated Efforts"
Awake!: April 22, 1996, pp. 4-7 "Who Can Bring
Lasting Peace?"
Awake!: November 22, 1998, pp. 3-14, Series of
Articles
Awake!: June 8, 1999, pp. 5-6, "Avoid Trauma"
subheading
Awake!: December 8, 2000, pp. 3-12, Series of
Articles

Now, although the Watchtower Society had been publishing small little blurbs about UN programs and such before their membership, it is interesting to note that they began publishing full articles – sometimes series of articles – about the UN, after their membership began. This revealed that they actually did know the requirements involved in membership! What's more, their claimed membership on the grounds of library access falls flat on its face because after they discontinued membership they continued to be able to publish information they gleaned from the UN library!

I saw it clearly: The Watchtower Organization was feigning innocence and ignorance. They weren't attempting to repent from their wrongs against the membership; instead they were trying to cover their tracks. I was stunned, broken, I didn't know what to do. I was born and raised believing that The Organization was God's sole channel for communication with mankind. They had *The* Truth! Although their boring and dry literature didn't suit me, up until this point I had still believed they were led by God's Holy Spirit and spoke for God!

My husband, God bless him, was very supportive of my crisis of faith. For three days I kept re-reading all the evidence I dug up, trying to find something that I might have missed which could exonerate The Watchtower Society. I blabbered on about it, walked around in a mental daze. Everything I ever believed and was taught was now called into question.

If they deceived us about this, what *else* have they done?!

My whole life I was taught they they were the only ones who could understand scripture, and I swallowed whatever scriptural "truths" they fed me without question. Even if I didn't understand their teaching (especially with prophecies), I always "waited on Jehovah" to help me understand – after all, these men in Bethel are spirit filled, they obviously knew more than I did, right?!

The scales fell off my eyes. I would no longer blindly accept whatever anyone said, I would only accept what the Bible actually says, and nothing else. I prayed to God like I'd never prayed before: Father, I am broken and lost. Everything I was ever taught is now a big question. I still believe in You, Your Son Jesus Christ, and the Bible. I am not listening to anyone right now, except for you. You I trust, I trust no one else. Teach me Your truth. Show me what's real.

I was now a newborn babe in Christ. And I had to save my parents and siblings from the lies and deceit of the Watchtower Society publications. I knew this would mean only trouble, but I had to give it my best shot. They needed to know these things too.

Chapter 13
My Exit

I started with my brother, Forrest. I showed him everything I found out about the NGO scandal. Looking back, I should have taken the time to think this through a little more, I know that now. But at the time, I didn't know how to handle *any* of this; all I knew is that my family needed to be warned!

Forrest was shocked at what I showed him. We discussed it, re-read the documentations, and discussed it some more. A few days later, I approached my mother with the same evidence. She immediately began making rationalizations as to why it must have been right for The Organization to do these things. She didn't see anything wrong with the UN Charter, despite the Watchtower Organization's published statements that they were a *"confederacy against God"* and a *"conspiracy against divine rule"*. In her mind, if they did something, it had to be right even if she didn't understand it. I tried showing her the evidence against their Library Card claims, but she didn't even want to look at it. I'd hit a brick wall with her, so I decided not to push it, figuring I could re-approach the topic with her another time. I also held off on telling my other siblings for the moment as I knew this was something that needed to be done more carefully: Forrest seemed pretty open to the situation, but Dad and Mom weren't, I had to be careful that the rest of the family didn't shut me out as an "apostate"; because once that happened, nothing I could say would get through.

Meanwhile, I spent my time digging deep into the Bible. My free time was consumed with comparing what the Bible said with what the Watchtower literature said, and I began to realize why their unique interpretations of prophecy were always so hard to grasp – their interpretations were a hodge-podge of unrelated scriptures strung together to look like something they weren't. I also began to see how the

Watchtower publications would forbid things that weren't really forbidden in scripture, and require things that also weren't required in scripture. They would "strain out the gnat but gulp down the camel" (*Matthew 23:24*), much like the Pharisees did.

As I read the Bible compared to the Watchtower study materials, I began to see how they used scriptures out of context and added meanings that weren't originally there. I also started noticing how the Watchtower Organization resorted to mis-quoting people in their publications, manipulating the quotes in order to make the them sound as if they supported the Jehovah's Witness point of view when in reality they didn't. It was enlightening and horrifying at the same time. Realize, I wasn't looking for fault, I was actually searching to see what was *right* in their doctrine; and though I did find that they had some things right, I was also discovering that they had an incredible amount of doctrine that was just plain wrong.

Being that I had been living my whole life as a Jehovah's Witness, I was struggling with figuring out what to do, as my faith was being completely overhauled. But, since I didn't really know what else to do at the time, I continued to attend meetings at the Kingdom Hall and continued to go out in Field Service. However, as I began learning real bible truth, I found myself disliking the Service work more and more; I didn't want to be teaching householders the doctrines that I didn't agree with.

Therefore, I came to decide that when I went out in Service I wouldn't offer the Watchtower literature for a Bible study anymore. Instead I would simply offer the householders The Bible. The first time I tried this was also the last time I ever went out in Service:

I was in a car group with three sisters and the young son of one of the sisters. The son noticed that I only had Bibles in my book bag and no other literature. He was probably only about seven years old, but he was already very indoctrinated: When I explained that my plan was to simply offer Bibles for a Bible study, he exclaimed "You can't have a Bible study with just a Bible!" Everyone else in the car agreed. In spite of their opinions, I continued on offering just the Bible to the householders. None of the women in my car group was impressed. That's when I decided I wasn't going to go out in Service ever again; I simply could not bring myself to teach people the many doctrines that I no longer agreed with. Since a publisher is required to teach *all* the doctrines to their Bible studies, I knew I would just have to abandon the activity.

In the meantime, I was still holding personal Bible studies with my children, and I also began to create a website based on the things I was learning from the Bible. I guess it was my way of trying to work out the truth from the lies; and I wanted it online so I could access the information from anywhere: Home, public libraries, Internet cafes, etc. I also became a member of an ex-Jehovah's Witness discussion forum online so that I could discuss scriptures with others who had experienced my situation; I was still trying to figure out fact from fiction.

I was acutely aware that my awakening to real truth would put my status in the Kingdom Hall in jeopardy. Currently, I was a member in good standing, but I knew that if I didn't handle things right, I'd be rejected as an apostate, the equivalent of spiritual poison. At the same time, though, I couldn't just nod my head and go along with whatever they said. Their doctrines of salvation, communion, and "truth" were dangerous and crippling from a spiritual viewpoint. People needed to know what's wrong within the Jehovah's Witness teachings, my family needed to know. I was between the proverbial rock and a hard place.

Sometime during this, I started showing Forrest the Bible website I was building. He thought it was put together well and read some of the articles that I wrote. I began to think that maybe I was getting through to him, though I still didn't try to push him. Well, I was wrong: Without saying a word to me, he went behind my back and showed our parents and the Elders my website. I had no clue of this until the Elders showed up at my door step with print offs from my website. Now, I was not ashamed of my site, and I wasn't angry that Forrest disagreed with it. However, I was a bit upset that he didn't have the courage to tell me he was uncomfortable with this stuff and that he felt the need to say something to the Elders about it. Sure, I would have been disappointed, but I would have understood and would have left him alone about it.

The Elders ran a battery of questions at me: Is this your site? Are you writing these things? Who is teaching you this stuff?

I admitted it was my site and that I was writing the information. They wouldn't believe me when I insisted that I was getting the information on my own; they insisted that I must be talking to other apostates who are filling my head with "lies". I guess they didn't think I was intelligent enough to investigate or think for myself. I mean, yes, I was looking at a message forum online, and yes I was involved in some discussions, however I always let the Bible have the final say – I didn't just swallow what others told me. I'd already had enough of that the previous thirty-six years!

When I tried to explain that I had prayed and asked God to give me wisdom and help me understand real truth from the scriptures, they misconstrued my words. As a result, they told my family that I claimed to be a special prophet of some kind and that I believed that God spoke directly to me. I just rolled my eyes when I heard about that later.

Since they believe that God speaks only through the Organization, and that the Bible was written only for the anointed ones, and that God doesn't just give knowledge to anyone, they didn't believe that God would directly teach me anything of value. Of course, their views on this are unbiblical, since scriptures clearly states that God does indeed give to anyone who asks (*Matthew 7:7-8, 21:22*).

Anyway, they insisted that I needed to take my website down because, in their view, I was teaching untruth on the site. So I asked them to show me *from scripture* what things I had wrong on the site. Since all Jehovah's Witness doctrine is supposed to be Bible based, then they should have been able to show me from scripture where I'm wrong. Instead, they tried to show me through the *Watchtower Organization's publications*. Again, I asked for *biblical* references, yet they refused. I informed them that I wasn't trying to be a troublemaker, but that I simply couldn't bridge some of the Bible's words with some of the Jehovah's Witness teachings, and I simply wanted someone to show me the connections from the Bible. Again, they wouldn't. I was labeled as being argumentative. I told them that I couldn't go out in Service and teach things that I didn't believe were true. One of the Elders retorted: "If the Organization says I have to preach that the tree is orange, when really it's green, I'm still gonna preach that it's orange! The Organization gives us directions, and that's what we do in the name of unity!"

I was flabbergasted.

Somewhere along the line in conversation the NGO scandal came up. Apparently, Forrest and Mom had told the Elders about my research on that too. I brought out all the evidence I had about it. They wouldn't even look at it. Instead, they took turns bombing me with scriptures and doctrine that was in favor of the Watchtower Organization, and I was not allowed to finish a single thought whenever I tried to respond. At one point, I got insistent and pointed out to them that they were telling me everything and that they weren't willing to look at my side. They agreed finally to look at what I had, took a two second look, and resumed bombing me with scriptures and doctrine again. I felt like a bird circling a tree, not being able to land anywhere. It was obvious that they already had their minds made up: I was wrong, they were right, and nothing else was going to get through.

After a couple of hours they finally left, satisfied that they did what they could to save me. I'd felt like I'd just gone through a major battle.

Right after this meeting, my family's attitude towards me began to change. We had an online family website I had started years earlier in which we could chat, write messages, share photos and whatnot. Being a Jehovah's Witness family, many of the topics for discussion were faith related. I was careful to respond in neutral ways, but no matter what I said, they were now starting to take me all wrong. For example, one family member started a topic in which we could all tell what our favorite scripture is. I simply put my scripture as *2 Timothy 3:16-17*, which says *"All scripture is inspired of God and beneficial for teaching, for reproving, for setting things straight, for disciplining in righteousness, that the man of God may be fully competent, completely equipped for every good work"*. It had been my favorite scripture for years, it wasn't something new. In fact, my mother even made me a plastic canvass cover for my Daily Text devotional with that very scripture reference on it some years before. Anyway, in the context of my "weakened faith", they took it all wrong and decided I was trying to make some kind of veiled reference to my recent Bible research. I couldn't win. So I tried limiting my responses to topics that weren't specifically faith based.

They tolerated my presence on the family site for some time, though it was becoming apparent that I wasn't going to take down my Bible website. This, of course, started causing questions. I tried to answer as unoffensively as I could, but the only answers they wanted would involve my re-conformity to the Jehovah's Witnesses. It got to the point that nobody wanted to talk to me on the family site. I knew my disfellowshipping was on the horizon, so I relinquished the family website to my brother, Joe, to administrate. I knew nobody would want to come to the website anymore if I were still the administrator *and* disfellowshipped. Despite their views of me, the family was spread across the United States and Canada, meaning that the family site was a good way for everyone to stay in touch with each other, and I didn't want to ruin that for them.

Although I saw the disfellowshipping coming, I didn't want to be disfellowshipped because I didn't want to lose association with my family. So I tried to stay under the radar as long as I could, though I continued to build my website. Unfortunately, the Elders were keeping track of me *and* my site. They finally concluded that I was an unrepentant apostate and they began taking steps towards disfellowshipping me if I didn't take the site down immediately. I couldn't bring myself to do it because I felt that by doing so I would be denying all the things God was opening my eyes to. I refused. They responded that I had to appear before the Judicial Committee. I agreed and we arranged a time to meet.

A Judicial Committee is the prescribed formality outlined by The Watchtower Organization during the process of a disfellowshipping. A Judicial Committee is made up of three Elders from my own congregation, plus me, and takes place in a little room within the Kingdom Hall. It wasn't mandatory for me to attend this meeting, for they could hold the committee with or without me. However, I did want one final time to speak my peace, and perhaps plant a few seeds in the minds of the Elders, so I chose to attend.

Now, part of the rules of the Judicial Committee includes not bringing in any recording devices, and nobody else can be in the room besides the Elders and myself (unless there was a witness in my defense). I played nice and didn't bring a recording device, and my husband waited in a separate area. For once, they actually let me say everything that I wanted to say. They pulled out the copies of my web site pages, and then proceeded to pick them apart. They were appalled that I recommended using just a Bible instead of the Watchtower in the door-to-door work. They thought it was incredible that I was telling people that anyone can receive wisdom from God simply by asking for it. They couldn't believe I was openly disagreeing with their doctrine of 1914. In response, I stuck to my guns and continued to ask them for biblical evidence that I was wrong. Again, they refused to do so (mainly because they couldn't). I told them I couldn't go door-to-door teaching things that wasn't backed up with scripture. They told me that it wasn't up to me to decide what scripture said, it was up to The Organization. After about an hour of back-and-forth conversation, they made the decision to disfellowship me. I immediately responded that I wanted to appear before an Appeals Committee.

An "Appeals Committee" is a special meeting for those who wish to appeal the decision of disfellowshipping. While awaiting your Appeals Committee meeting they cannot formally disfellowship you, though you will be put on restrictions during the meantime. It was going to break my parents' hearts to be disfellowshipped, as they would believe that it's basically a death sentence. This appeal bought me a little bit of time.

An Appeals Committee is made up of three Elders from a *different* congregation, as well as the three Elders who were at my Judicial Committee meeting, and myself. My Appeals Committee was arranged within two weeks.

The Appeals Committee started out with me and the three other Elders getting to know each other a little for a few minutes. Then they got down to business. They briefly reviewed what happened at my Judicial Committee, and looked at the evidence from both sides. These three other Elders came across as cold and robotic; akin to Stepford Elders. I tried my case again. At one point, they questioned why I thought I should know something that the Governing Body didn't know, since they were more educated than I was. I simply responded that all I had to know was how to read, and I was reading the Bible. They also informed me that my website would "stumble" other Jehovah's Witnesses, therefore I should be disfellowshipped. My response? *"What about The Organization??!! They stumbled ME, and they aren't getting disfellowshipped!"* They countered with *"Jehovah will deal with them if that's the case",* in which I further responded *"If Jehovah can deal with them, then why can't He just deal with me too, instead of disfellowshipping me??!!"*

Well, for some reason, it was different for them than for me. And besides that, they felt I was trying to draw away the others in the congregation as well. I reminded them that I wasn't talking to other congregants so to speak, I had only been speaking to my own family; one of which was a Ministerial Servant and one of which was an actual Elder out of state.

After what seemed like an endless session of discussion, questions, responses and so forth they sent me out of the room to make their decision. I waited an entire twenty minutes before they called me back in. You have to understand, twenty minutes is a very long time for such a decision, as usually these types of decisions are made in less than five. As the time ticked on, I was bursting with curiosity as to why it was taking so long – were they taking the time to review my documentation? Were they considering the possibility that some of the things I had been learning are actually right? Who knows; and I will never know. All I know is that they finally called me back into the room and told me that I was going to be disfellowshipped. The one Stepford Elder unbelievably said to me "We aren't doing this to punish you, we are doing this because we love you", and he said it with all the emotion of a stone. I felt like screaming "you can't possibly love me because you don't even know me!", but I restrained myself.

According to Watchtower policy, my disfellowshipping was to be announced in seven days.

My husband brought me back home, and I immediately went online to break the news to my family. I totally saw it coming, and I could only hold it off for so long, and now was the moment I dreaded – losing them all. So I went on the family site and wrote my message. I wanted Dad and Mom to have a few days to get through the initial raw emotions before hearing it announced at the meeting. In their eyes, being disfellowshipped as an apostate was the worst thing – tons worse than being disfellowshipped for smoking cigarettes. In the Jehovah's Witness world, an apostate is an enemy of

Jehovah, is a liar, and has committed the unforgivable sin of blaspheming the Holy Spirit. I was as good as dead and rejected by Jehovah, in their eyes.

That entire week my family kept contact with me. According to the "rules" I wasn't truly disfellowshipped until the actual announcement took place, so at least I was able to make some sort of peace with my family before the official announcement took place.

At this time I decided I would no longer attend meetings at the Kingdom Hall, as I had no more reason to continue going there. I wouldn't be able to socialize with my family or friends in the congregation, and I certainly hadn't been going in order to hear the doctrine over the past several months. I had taken my stand for God, went through the grinder for it, and now it was completely finished. There was no point in continuing to attend the meetings anymore, so I simply didn't go to any more of them. Therefore, I was not present at the meeting when my disfellowshipping was announced.

I never set foot in a Kingdom Hall again after this.

Chapter 14
A New Beginning

I was disfellowshipped just before Thanksgiving of 2004. At this point I was glad that my husband never became a Jehovah's Witness because if he had, he would have had his own dilemmas with this entire situation: IF he were a Jehovah's Witness, and also disagreed with the information I was finding, it would have caused a major rift in our marriage. In the Jehovah's Witness world, you are allowed to leave your spouse if you are facing "spiritual endangerment". Being that I was viewed as an apostate, I would have fit in the "spiritual endangerment" category, and he could have possibly considered leaving me, if he were one of them. A vile apostate like me could lure him away from The Truth, jeopardizing his entrance into the New Order. Alternatively, if he was a member and *did* happen to agree with my findings, he would have also been disfellowshipped right along with me. However, since in reality he was never a Jehovah's Witness to begin with, they view him as simply being unlearned and not knowing any better – which wouldn't be his fault (since it would have been up to me to teach him). Because he was simply ignorant of The Truth, he was not to be shunned in contrast to ME, who knew better but left.

Of course, my husband didn't attend the Kingdom Hall meetings with me anyway, so it's not like he had any friends there to be concerned about. The biggest issue was my family ties: They could associate with *him*, they just couldn't associate with me. As for our children, they were likewise acceptable too, since they had never been baptized into the faith yet. As I stated before, one's baptism changes one's position in the congregation. Before baptism you are viewed as not being fully knowledgeable of The Truth. After baptism you are viewed as having full knowledge of The Truth (especially since you've answered all the baptismal questions correctly), and therefore should know better than to leave it.

Thus, our children were viewed as "unknowledgeable" since they hadn't yet been baptized. You can't fault a person for being unlearned (again, that fault would have been laid on *me*), and so they are not shunned. Therefore, my family members could still have association with my husband and children any time. This didn't matter very much though because they were never invited anywhere by them. However, to this day, if we happen to see them in the supermarket, my husband and children can go over to say "hi" and chit chat with them without causing a stir.

Losing the association with my family is the only part of being disfellowshipped that I don't like. Before my disfellowshipping, my mother and I talked on the phone every day, I visited the family web site every day, and frequently visited the family members who still lived in the area. Now that was all gone. My husband's family all lived a couple hours away, so it wasn't feasible to see them on a daily basis. Being a Jehovah's Witness all my life, I wasn't exactly bursting at the seams with non-believing friends, so I was in a tough spot, socially speaking. I did have one co-worker, Elaine, whom I started befriending. She lived within walking distance of my home and had kids about the same age as my kids. She was a Christian who once studied with Jehovah's Witnesses in the past, so I was able to talk to her about a lot of the stuff I had been going through – it was a blessing! Beyond her, I didn't seek out any other friendships at the time. I was still busy in my free time reading the bible and learning what real Christianity was all about. After thirty-six years of indoctrination into The Watchtower Organization, it was going to take a while to sift through the falsehoods and build a solid faith on *real* truth.

As I learned new things, I was finding a new freedom. No longer was I chained to doctrines that I didn't understand. No longer was I required to go along with endless rules for the sake of unity. No longer was I tied to letting others do my thinking for me. I was free to grow in Christ at my own pace, and it felt WONDERFUL!

As I continued to learn things I kept adding information to my bible website. Because I was so new to real Christianity, I found myself constantly revising the information that I posted because I had a lot of <u>un</u>learning to do. I'll be the first to admit that, even though I was seeing with newly opened eyes, it's still a very difficult thing to shed a life-time's worth of false teachings. I would visit and re-visit various bible topics just to be sure that I was understanding things correctly. It took me a couple of years to undo the majority of my Jehovah's Witness indoctrination. And, to this day, I *still* catch myself contending with a "hang-up" every once in a while. I'm sure this will be a lifelong process indeed.

In the meantime, God has been very giving and very patient towards me. I know I'll never be a perfect Christian who gets it 100% correct because I tend to get in my own way all the time. However, I don't let that discourage me; I am free to grow, free to question, and free to ask God for anything I need. Although He doesn't owe me anything, He has been so good to me, and He has been blessing me the whole time in spite of myself.

Praise God for His immeasurable love and mercy!

Chapter 15
Continuing Forward

A little more than a year after my disfellowshipping, I began to realize how much I was missing out on congregational fellowship. Although my personal bible study was doing lots of good things for me, I was still missing out on a social life, and the children weren't getting a solid Christian social life either. I decided it was time to start exploring our local churches.

I was pretty particular about which church to try. I wanted to stay clear of overly-controlling   denominations; I wanted one in which we could experience real, individual, spiritual growth. We'd seen commercials on television for the United Church of Christ and decided to try them first. They were advertising their acceptance of anyone who came through their doors regardless of background, and we kinda liked the idea. So we found a local congregation, bundled up on the next Sunday morning, and we all went to the church. We arrived at the little white church where an usher seated us. Attendance was a little sparse, but perhaps it was due to the frigid winter weather that day.

It wasn't too awfully strange for me to walk into a church. This was because, during a my rocky teens years before my baptism, I was sent to live in an all-girl group home for eighteen months. You see, by the time I'd hit my teen years I was yearning for more freedoms than the Jehovah's Witness allowed and started acting out. I wanted to date boys at my school, attend the school games and dances, dress in clothes that my mother didn't pick out for me. Even though I still believed in the Jehovah's Witness doctrines, I wanted to have a normal teen life like everyone else, and the only way to do it was to sneak around. I began to runaway from home, skip school to hang out with classmates and come home late. Ultimately, my behavior resulted in my stay at the group home for teen girls. All the girls in the group home were required to attend some kind of worship service each week, so I went with the staff members to their churches. Because I had been sent to the Group Home, I was too embarrassed to show my face at the Kingdom Hall – what a reproach I had brought upon Jehovah! But since I couldn't be left all by myself at the group home on Sundays, I opted to go to the staff members' churches. Mostly I'd just sit in a side room outside the sanctuary and just wait for the service to be over. Sometimes though, the room would be unavailable, so I'd sit in on the church service in the sanctuary, which made me a little uncomfortable, but I had no choice. During my year and a half at the group home I had been in a variety of churches, therefore I had an idea of what to expect when I walked into this church on this particular winter morning.

When my family and I entered that church, we didn't feel "it". Nobody greeted us except for the usher. The pastor didn't seem to be very enthused about his own sermon, and the atmosphere was void of the feeling of Spirit and brotherhood. We never returned to that congregation again.

A few months later some Mormons came to our door. Although I knew I didn't want to be a Mormon, I accepted their invitation to attend their church service because I was curious as to how they "did" church. A young Mormon couple picked me up the following Sunday and brought me to their church. The people there were very friendly, and there was a lot of warmth flowing amongst the members. The service had lots of testimonials, lots of talk from the Book of Mormon, and a communion consisting of plain water and bread. Although I thoroughly enjoyed the friendliness of the congregation, I knew there was just too many things I disagreed with in their doctrines. My curiosity was satisfied, and I declined further invitations to attend their services.

It was a few more months before I started getting really serious about finding a church. I started praying to God, looking for His guidance in finding a church home suitable for our family. I looked online at local church web sites and liked one in particular: It was an inter-denominational congregation (Presbyterian & American Baptist) It had a midweek youth club which included bible study, activities and supper, and a Thursday night teen group that also had bible study, activities, and supper. This church also offered many other fellowship opportunities: Knitting groups, a weekly exercise group, missions activities, weekly bible studies and *more*! I made up my mind to attend a service the next Sunday, which happened to be Christmas Eve. This was now just over two years after my disfellowshipping.

The church was in walking distance, and I went by myself. I seated myself in a pew towards the back and took a good look around: This church was old and it was large. It featured high ceilings, tall stained glass windows, and a seated balcony section. The chancel was decorated for Christmas, and everyone was so friendly! There must have been more than two hundred people already there, but in spite of the crowd the visitation ministers – a married couple – noticed me right away and came to welcome me. We chit-chatted for a few minutes until the starting music came on. The pews all had Bibles available – I liked that. Pastor Jim came up to the pulpit to start the service. I liked that he was dressed in a regular suit and tie instead of the showy robes that many church leaders wear. He was a slender, middle aged man sporting a beard and glasses, and seemed very down-to-earth.

The service included Bible readings, choir music, a children's time and an engaging sermon. I loved the warmth and friendliness, the inclusion of bible readings, the time for children, and the fact that the Pastor didn't put on a showy display of grandeur. I was totally smitten with this congregation! The following Sunday I brought my husband and the kids with me, and that was the beginning of our relationship with that congregation. The kids blossomed with the children and teen programs, I joined a bible study and a women's group, started volunteering for the Youth Club and got to know quite a few people in the congregation. Ten months later I decided to join this church – I had found a good spiritual home!

Since my church congregation is located right in the middle of town, I knew that sooner or later some of my family members would see me either coming or going from the church building (especially since I was involved in so many church activities). I also knew that when any of them saw me entering or exiting the building, there would be a vicious rumor mill circling about me on the family website. After much consideration, I decided I should write individual letters to each family member detailing my situation. That way, at least, everyone would know the same facts, perhaps tempering the invention of fiction.

My letter wasn't mean or sarcastic. I simply let them know that we had been attending that particular church and the different programs which I was involved in. I explained that I knew they wouldn't agree with my choice, and that I simply wanted everyone to have their facts straight if any of them should happen to see me coming or going from the church. I reiterated that I wasn't planning to return to the Jehovah's Witnesses as many of my new found beliefs do not agree with them. I knew it wasn't going to be the happiest letter for them to receive, but I did want them to have the correct information straight from me. I didn't try to preach to them, I didn't try to get them to accept my choices, I simply gave them information on my situation in case they noticed me hanging around the church. They each got a copy of the same exact letter.

Quentin called me on the phone a couple of days later and informed me that the family website was all abuzz about my letters! Apparently, Dad and Mom got their letter first, and proceeded to tell everyone to throw away their copies, that I had joined a church, and that my letters were full of apostate stuff so don't bother reading them!. They were deciding that I was trying to lure them away, trying to spread my apostasy to them, and whatever. Amelia put "return to sender" on her copy, with a note written on it saying "DO NOT write to me ever again!".

Good grief – they were all so afraid of the letter! I hadn't been trying to convince them of doctrine or anything, yet they were so *terrified*; it was unbelievable! I couldn't get over how scared they were over the information, it wasn't like I was trying to convert them or anything. But whatever, I just let it blow over and said nothing more after that.

In the meantime, I kept myself busy exploring Christianity from a church point of view. My congregation held adult Sunday school classes at the same time the children had theirs, and so I started attending them. Every few weeks they'd start a different series of classes, and there was always two or three classes to choose from – I really appreciated having the option to choose for myself! And, what really blew me away was that in all of the classes it was *expected* that attendees would have differing points of view! You *could* have differing opinions on what a symbolic bible passage meant. You *could* have a different opinion on what a bible character was thinking during a major event. You *could* ask questions if you didn't understand or agree with what someone's point of view. This was all new to me – and it was great!

And it didn't stop there! Although certain core beliefs were assumed (The Bible is true, Jesus is the Saviour, God is the Father, Satan is the enemy, etc.), you were free to develop your relationship with God on your own level. You didn't have to all be learning the exact same thing at the exact same time. You weren't ostracized for reading literature published by a different church. You weren't ostracized if you *visited* another church! You could start your own bible study groups if you wanted. Within bible study groups, you could comment any way you liked – you weren't tethered to a rote formula!

Oh, I'm sure plenty of churches are like mine, and that's the beauty of it – so many people can experience this same freedom in Christ, just like I was discovering!

And not only that, but I was also discovering something *else* I wasn't even looking for: How many lies The Organization told me about churches. For example, one of the biggest things The Organization teaches is that all churches promote the Father, the Son, and the Holy Spirit are the very same singular being. However, I was now learning that only *some* denominations teach that – it isn't a universal doctrine amongst the churches. I was also taught that churches don't use the name "Jehovah", and yet here I was seeing that very name in the church hymnals *and* hearing it in some of the sermons – I was even hearing the name at times in Christian songs on the Christian radio station! I was also taught that no other church performs a continuous door-to-door preaching program, yet here I was finding some local churches (non-Mormon, by the way) who *do* actually have such continuous programs!

I was amazed at how much I was learning, and I was vexed at how many untruths I was taught all my life. Thank you God, for taking the blinders off me!

Chapter 16
Life in Christ

Although I still miss the companionship of my Jehovah's Witness family members, the initial hurt has lost much of its sting over time. I continue to pray for them though, that they too will be able to see past their blinders and allow God to direct their paths. In the meantime, I have no regrets for the path that I have taken. I have come to know Christ in a way that simply wasn't possible during my time as a Jehovah's Witness, and for that I am eternally grateful. I treasure the fellowship of my church family, and I thoroughly enjoy the freedoms we have in Christ. Amen and Hallelujah.

If you know of anyone who is studying with the Jehovah's Witnesses, or if you know a Jehovah's Witness who is beginning to question the doctrine, do them a big favor and pray for their deliverance from the sect. Please be supportive of their situations, as the process of leaving the Jehovah's Witnesses is long and hard, especially when one has family members still in the sect. Be there for them, they will need your support.

INTRODUCTION TO THE APPENDICES

The following series of appendices explores various topics
unique to the Jehovah's Witnesses culture and mindset. I've
added this section because we believe it has value in educating
the public about this sect.

Appendix 1: The 1975 Debacle

Many are familiar with the 1975 debacle. For those who don't know, in the latter half of the 1960's, Watchtower publications began publishing information that strongly led readers into believing that 1975 was the year Armageddon was going to occur. Here are some examples of what they published:

> <u>Yes, the end of this system is so very near! Is that not reason to increase our activity? In this regard we can learn something from a runner who puts on a final burst of speed near the finish of a race. Look at Jesus, who apparently stepped up his activity during his final days on earth. In fact, over 27 percent of the material in the Gospels is devoted to just the last week of Jesus' earthly ministry!—</u> Matt. 21:1-27:50; Mark 11:1-15:37; Luke 19:29-23:46; John 11:55-19:30. By carefully and prayerfully examining our own circumstances, we also may find that we can <u>spend more time and energy in preaching during this final period before the present system ends.</u> Many of our brothers and sisters are doing just that. This is evident from the rapidly increasing number of pioneers. Yes, since the summer of 1973 there have been new peaks in pioneers every month. Now there are 20,394 regular and special pioneers in the United States, an all-time peak. That is 5,190 more than there were in February 1973! A 34-percent increase! Does that not warm our hearts? <u>Reports are heard of brothers selling their homes and property and planning to finish out the rest of their days in this old system in the pioneer service. Certainly this is a fine way to spend the short time remaining before the wicked world's end.</u>—1 John 2:17. **Our Kingdom Ministry May 1974 p.3 How Are You Using Your Life?**

That work of liberation and salvation must go on to the finish! To give aid today in this critical time to prospective sons of God," announced President Knorr, "a new book in English, entitled 'Life Everlasting-in Freedom of the Sons of God,' has been published." At all assembly points where it was released, the book was received enthusiastically. Crowds gathered around stands and soon supplies of the *book were depleted. Immediately its contents were examined. It did not take the brothers very long to find the chart beginning on page 31, showing that 6,000 years of man's existence end in 1975. Discussion of 1975 overshadowed about everything else. "The new book compels us to realize that Armageddon is, in fact, very close indeed," said a conventioner.* **The Watchtower 1966 October 15 pp.628-9 Rejoicing over "God's Sons of Liberty" Spiritual Feast**

So in not many years within our own generation we are reaching what Jehovah God could view as the seventh day of man's existence. How appropriate it would be for Jehovah God to make of this coming seventh period of a thousand years a sabbath period of rest and release, a great Jubilee sabbath for the proclaiming of liberty throughout the earth to all its inhabitants! This would be most timely for mankind. It would also be most fitting on God's part, for, remember, mankind has yet ahead of it what the last book of the Holy Bible speaks of as the reign of Jesus Christ over earth for a thousand years, the millennial reign of Christ. Prophetically Jesus Christ, when on earth nineteen centuries ago, said concerning himself: "For Lord of the sabbath is what the Son of man is." (Matthew 12: 8). It would not be by mere chance or accident but would be according to the loving purpose of Jehovah God for the reign of Jesus Christ, the 'Lord of the Sabbath,' to run parallel with the seventh millennium of man's existence. **Life Everlasting in Freedom of the Sons of God (book) 1966 pp. 29-30**

6,000 Years Completed in 1975 ... In what year, then, would the first 6,000 years of man's existence and also the first 6,000 years of God's rest day come to an end? The year 1975... Hence, the fact that we are nearing the end of the first 6,000 years of man's existence is of great significance. Does God's rest day parallel the time man has been on earth since his creation? Apparently so. From the most reliable investigations of Bible chronology, harmonizing with many accepted dates of secular history, we find that Adam was created in the autumn of the year 4026 B.C.E. Sometime in that same year Eve could well have been created, directly after which God's rest day commenced ... There is another chronological indication that we are rapidly nearing the closing time for this wicked system of things. It is the fact that shortly, according to reliable Bible chronology, 6,000 years of human history will come to an end.. After six thousand years of toil and bondage to sin, sickness, death and Satan, mankind is due to enjoy a rest and is in dire need of a rest. (Heb. 4:1-11) Hence, the fact that we are nearing the end of the first 6,000 years of man's existence is of great significance.. In what year, then, would the first 6,000 years of man's existence and also the first 6,000 years of God's rest day come to an end? The year 1975. This is worthy of notice, particularly in view of the fact that the 'last days' began in 1914, and that the physical facts of our day in fulfillment of prophecy mark this as the last generation of this wicked world. So we can expect the immediate future to be filled with thrilling events for those who rest their faith in God and his promises. It means that within relatively few years we will witness the fulfillment of the remaining prophecies that have to do with the 'time of the end.' **Awake! October 8 1966 pp.19-20**

But, without a doubt, nothing has created more interest in this textbook than the first chapter with its chart and fine information regarding the 7,000 years of God's rest day. The observation that 1975 may well mark the beginning of mankind's great Jubilee has intrigued many. **The Watchtower 1967 January 1 p.28**

Making some special effort to do more than the usual helps us live up to our dedication. In view of the short period of time left, we want to do this as often as circumstances permit. Just think, brothers, there are only about ninety months left before 6,000 years of man's existence on earth is completed... Do you remember what we learned at the assemblies last summer? The majority of people living today will probably be alive when Armageddon breaks out, and there are no resurrection hopes for those who are destroyed then. So, now more than ever, it is vital not to ignore that spirit of wanting to do more. **Our Kingdom Ministry March 1968 p.4**

After 6,000 years of misery, toil, trouble, sickness and death under Satan's rule, mankind is indeed in dire need of relief, a rest. The seventh day of the Jewish week, the sabbath, would well picture the final 1,000-year reign of God's kingdom under Christ when mankind would be uplifted from 6,000 years of sin and death. (Rev. 20:6) Hence, when Christians note from God's timetable the approaching end of 6,000 years of human history, it fills them with anticipation. Particularly is this true because the great sign of the "last days" has been in the course of fulfillment since the beginning of the "time of the end" in 1914. And, as Jesus said, "this generation will by no means pass away until all these things occur." **The Watchtower 1968 May 1 pp.271-3, para. 6, Making Wise Use of the Remaining Time**

6,000 Years Nearing Completion [...] The fact that fifty-four years of the period called the 'last days' have already gone by is highly significant. It means that only a few years, at most, remain before the corrupt system of things dominating the earth is destroyed by God. **Awake! October 8 1968 pp. 14-15**

If you are a young person, you also need to face the fact that you will never grow old in this present system of things. Why not? Because all the evidence in fulfillment of Bible prophecy indicates that this corrupt system is due to end in a few years. Of the generation that observed the beginning of the 'last days' in 1914, Jesus foretold: 'This generation will by no means pass away until all these things occur.' Therefore, as a young person, you will never fulfill any career that this system offers. If you are in high school and thinking about a college education, it means at least four, perhaps even six or eight more years to graduate into a specialized career. But where will this system of things be by that time? It will be well on the way towards its finish, if not actually gone! **Awake! 1969 May 22 p.15**

With such confident and adamant language, the worldwide membership of Jehovah's Witnesses had no choice but to believe they were being told that the "END!" was going to happen in the year 1975. What other way is there to take such information? Of course, in the midst of all this promotion, the Watchtower Society also published a back-up disclaimer from time to time, just in case they weren't exactly correct:

> *'What about the year 1975? What is it going to mean, dear friends?' asked Brother Franz. 'Does it mean that Armageddon is going to be finished, with Satan bound, by 1975? It could! It could! All things are possible with God. Does it mean that Babylon the Great is going to go down by 1975? It could. Does it mean that the attack of Gog of Magog is going to be made on Jehovah's witnesses to wipe them out, then Gog himself will be put out of action? It could. But we are not saying. All things are possible with God. But we are not saying. And don't any of you be specific in saying anything that is going to happen between now and 1975. But the big point of it all is this, dear friends: Time is short. Time is running out, no question about that.* **The Watchtower 1966 October 15 p.631 Rejoicing over "God's Sons of Liberty" Spiritual Feast**

> *The publications of Jehovah's witnesses have shown that, according to Bible chronology, it appears that 6,000 years of man's existence will be completed in the mid-1970's. But these publications have never said that the world's end would come then.* **The Watchtower 1974 October 15 p.635 Growing in Appreciation for the "Divine Purpose"**

> *The office in Czechoslovakia sent a letter dated February 22, 1972, to all congregations. It set out a lengthy explanation of reasons why we should not make any definite assertions about the date when Armageddon will strike. It pointed out that no publication of the Society had said that Armageddon will come in a certain year. The letter concluded: "Jehovah's Witnesses around the world are familiar with these facts, and no one should add any personal claims as to what will happen before or during the year 1975. There are no Scriptural grounds for any claims, and they could have a detrimental effect on the preaching work.*
> **Yearbook 2000 pp.196-7 Czech Republic**

Of course, these little disclaimers were few and far between during the 1975 furor, and were placed in among the information that was simultaneously promoting the End coming in 1975. I was only seven years old in the year 1975, but still I remember how, because the build-up of 1975 was so intense, most of the membership looked at these few disclaimers as nothing more than a formality. And when 1975 actually came and *went,* the Watchtower Society decided to add the membership to the blame of disappointment instead of keeping all of the blame on themselves:

> *It may be that some who have been serving God have planned their lives according to a mistaken view of just what was to happen on a certain date or in a certain year. They may have, for this reason, put off or neglected things that they otherwise would have cared for. But they have missed the point of the Bible's warnings concerning the end of this system of things, thinking that Bible chronology reveals the specific date.* **The Watchtower 1976 July 15 p.441, para. 11**

> *The brothers also appreciated the candor of this same talk, which acknowledged the Society's responsibility for some of the disappointment a number felt regarding 1975.* **1980 Yearbook of Jehovah's Witnesses pp.30-31**

> *With the appearance of the book Life Everlasting-in Freedom of the Sons of God, and its comments as to how appropriate it would be for the millennial reign of Christ to parallel the seventh millennium of man's existence, considerable expectation was aroused regarding the year 1975. There were statements made then, and thereafter, stressing that this was only a possibility. Unfortunately, however, along with such cautionary information, there were other statements published that implied that such realization of hopes by that year was more of a probability than a mere possibility. It is to be regretted that these latter statements apparently overshadowed the cautionary ones and contributed to a buildup of the expectation already initiated.*
> **The Watchtower 1980 March 15 pp.17-18 Choosing the Best Way of Life**

Bible Students, known since 1931 as Jehovah's Witnesses, also expected that the year 1925 would see the fulfillment of marvelous Bible prophecies. They surmised that at that time the earthly resurrection would begin, bringing back faithful men of old, such as Abraham, David, and Daniel. More recently, <u>many Witnesses conjectured that events associated with the beginning of Christ's Millennial Reign might start to take place in 1975</u>. Their anticipation was based on the understanding that the seventh millennium of human history would begin then. These erroneous views did not mean that God's promises were wrong, that he had made a mistake. By no means! The mistakes or misconceptions, as in the case of first-century Christians, were due to a failure to heed Jesus' caution, 'You do not know the time.' <u>The wrong conclusions were due, not to malice or to unfaithfulness to Christ, but to a fervent desire to realize the fulfillment of God's promises in their own time</u>.

Awake! 1995 June 22 p.9 Can You Trust God's Promises?

This particular fiasco in Jehovah's Witness teaching actually turned out to be a good thing: Many members left the sect because this failed teaching made them realize that it wasn't "Jehovah's Channel of Communication" after all.

Appendix 2: The 1914 Doctrine

The core doctrine of Jehovah's Witnesses is that Jesus Christ returned invisibly in 1914, what they call the "end of the seven Gentile times". They claim that the prophecy of a king's Nebuchadnezzar's dream in Daniel 4:10-17, (in which a tree was chopped down and banded for "seven times") coupled with the passage at Luke 21:24 (which states Jerusalem would be trampled on by the nations until the appointed times of the nations are fulfilled) point to the year of 1914.

(Note: I used "B.C." and "A.D.", whereas the Watchtower likes to us "B.C.E." and "C.E." respectively. However, both methods are interchangeable and do not alter the outcome of the math)

This is how they explain that (I tried to simplify this as much as possible):

> **1.** According to them, a prophetic "time" is synonymous with a literal year, as taken from Revelation 12:14
>
> **2.** According to them, a prophetic year is considered to be 360 days long.
>
> **3.** In Numbers 14:34, God counts each prophetic day as a literal year.
>
> **4.** The tree dream in Daniel mentions "seven times". This means: Seven times = seven years, which is 2,520 days. Since God prophetically counts days as years, this means 2,520 literal years.
>
> **5.** According to them, the passage in Luke 21:24 refers to the "times of the nations". Since the "nations" are spiritual Gentiles, this refers to the Gentile Times.

6. According to them, the Seven Gentile Times began in 607 BC, when God's Holy City of Jerusalem was destroyed by Babylon. Adding the 2,520 years to 607 BC comes up to the year 1914 AD.

Thus, according to them, this end of the "Seven Gentile Times" in 1914 was when Jesus Christ invisibly returned to seek out the "Faithful and Discreet Slave" referred to at *Matthew 24:45-47*. This Faithful and Discreet Slave would be the only group on earth dispensing proper spiritual food to people at the proper time (a.k.a. The Truth). According to them, Jesus saw that the Jehovah's Witnesses (who were called "Bible Students" at that time) were the only ones doing so, and thus they were blessed and appointed over all of the Master's spiritual belongings in 1919. (*"Worship God"*, ch.14, p. 130, par. 7-8) Thus, they believe they are the sole channel of true worship for mankind today.

Now, of course, there are several holes in this teaching; holes that I never saw before because I simply took their word for it all those years. Remember, Jehovah's Witnesses don't question The Organization because they believe that The Organization is Jehovah's Visible channel of communication. Even though I didn't really understand how they came to these conclusions regarding 1914, I obediently went along with it, "waiting on Jehovah" for understanding. Apparently my "waiting on Jehovah" paid off, because now I was looking into this doctrine with *opened* eyes, and I could clearly see the many problems with their explanation:

> 1. There is nothing in scripture that connects the tree dream in Daniel with Luke's "appointed times of the nations". NOTHING. The passage in Daniel with the tree dream prophesies the divine humbling of proud king Nebuchadnezzar of Babylon, whereas Christ's words in Luke foretold the destruction of Jerusalem by the Roman Empire – Two completely unrelated and unconnected events that were many centuries apart.

2.   Although The Society claims that **Daniel 4:17** (*God promises to give the Kingdom "to the one whom he wants to...even the lowliest of mankind*) refers to Jesus as receiving the Kingdom in 1914, in reality this scripture is simply referring to Nebuchadnezzar's beastly insanity that was soon to come upon him for seven years (as supported by **verses 16 and 33-34**). There is nothing here that connects to Jesus, the End Times, or the year 1914, yet The Watchtower Society applies it to these things anyway in their attempts to support their own doctrine.

3.   Christ's words in the Luke passage could not be pointed towards the Babylonian destruction of Jerusalem, since Christ was speaking of the *Roman* destruction. Yet The Society bends this around and attributes the beginning of the "Gentile Times" in Luke to mean the *Babylonian* destruction a Jerusalem, even though there are no scriptural passages that can tie these two events together.

4.   The book of Daniel explains the tree dream as representing king Nebuchadnezzar himself and nothing more (**Daniel 4:20-26**). Notably, whenever the book of Daniel reveals a prophecy pointing towards the End Times, it is always mentioned as such, *and* nowhere in the Book of Daniel is Nebuchadnezzar's tree dream mentioned as being one of the End Time prophecies.

5.   When researching the history of the Babylonian destruction of Jerusalem, the Watchtower Society is the *only* source that cites this as happening in **607 B.C**. Every other historical and archaeological source cites this event as happening in **586 B.C**.

6.   And, most interesting, is that the Watchtower Society's own publications have inadvertently agreed with the 586 BC date, even though they insistently continue to teach the 607 BC date.

That last point should be a real attention grabber, as it is oh so true. Let me lay it out for you:

1. According to their publication, **"Insight on the Scriptures"**, Volume 1, page 773, Babylon's king Nebuchadnezzar was succeeded by his son, Evil-Merodach.

According to the same publication, Volume 2, page 480, king Nebuchadnezzar reigned for 43 years before Evil-Merodach succeeded him.

2. *The Watchtower* Magazine of January 1, 1965, page 29 details the chronology in this manner: (a) Evil-Merodach (a.k.a. Awal-Marduk), reigned two years and was assassinated by (b) Neriglissar, who reigned for four years. Next, (c) Labashi-Marduk ascended the throne and was assassinated nine months later. It was after that (d) Nabonidus took the throne until Babylon fell in 539 BC, thus ending the line of Babylonian kings.

3. According to their publication *"Insight On the Scriptures"*, Volume 2, page 457, king Nabonidus ruled for a total of seventeen years, starting in 556 BC and ending in 539 BC.

Now, before adding this up, remember: When counting years **B**efore **C**hrist (B.C.) you're counting down the time to 1 AD because the BC numbers are counting the years before Christ....so the year "23 B.C." would mean "23 years before Christ's birth", the next year would be 22 years before Christ and would therefore be called "22 B.C." even though its the next year. With that being said, let's how the math works, according to their own publications:

Add up all the years of kingly reign:

1st -- Nebuchadnezzar : 43 years.
2nd-- Evil Merodach: 2 years
3rd-- Neriglissar: 4 years
4th-- Labashi-Marduk: 9 Months,
5th-- Nabonidus: 17 years

This is a total of 66.75 years of reign ending in 539 B.C.E. according to the Watchtower Society's own information. What year does this bring us to? 605 B.C. -- which agrees with other historical sources. Now, according to scripture, the first king on this list, Nebuchadnezzar, didn't destroy Jerusalem until his 18th year of reign (19th if you count his ascension year)

(*Jeremiah 32:1, 52:12*). Therefore, since Nebuchadnezzar was enthroned in 605 B.C.E., and took Jerusalem 18-19 years later, that puts the destruction of Jerusalem at 586/587 BC, which agrees with secular sources, and puts the dates *twenty years off* from the Watchtower's teaching of 607 BC! So if Jerusalem wasn't destroyed until 587, and the "Seven Gentile Times" ended 2,520 years later according to their reasoning, the Gentile Times wouldn't have ended in 1914, *they would have ended twenty years later in 1934!*

This twenty year difference is significant, as this would mean that the so-called "Gentile Times" *didn't* end in 1914, which means that Christ *didn't* come in 1914 to make his inspection, which means that he did not choose his "Faithful and Discreet Slave" in 1919, which further means that The Organization is *not* God's chosen channel for communication to mankind.

Using its own publications, the Watchtower has essentially destroyed its own core doctrine.

Appendix 3: Disfellowshipping In Scripture

The Jehovah's Witnesses tend to use a more extreme form of disfellowshipping than is outlined in the Bible. According to the Jehovah's Witness doctrine, a person who is disfellowshipped is not to be associated with, spoken to, or contacted except for in emergency situations. As for those living with a disfellowshipped family member, the Jehovah's Witness is to only to have normal day-to-day contact with the disfellowshipped one, forgoing any Bible study, prayer time, or recreational activities outside of the home. (***Our Kingdom Ministry***, *August 2002, p. 3 para. 6-7*).

Note that Scripture states:

> *For your part, brothers, do not give up in doing right. But if anyone is not obedient to our word through this letter, keep this one marked, stop associating with him, that he may become ashamed. And yet do not be considering him as an enemy, but continue admonishing him as a brother.*
> – *2Thessalonians 3:13-15*

In essence, this passage is saying YES, restrict the association, but still consider the person to be a Christian brother or sister and continue to admonish (advise) him or her. Jehovah's Witnesses, though, take this *further* and go on to restrict the person from acts of worship such as answering the questions in the study meetings, the full time door-to-door work, and other special privileges including the Theocratic Ministry School skits. I can understand the restriction of association due to the fact that *"Bad associations spoil useful habits" (1 Corinthians 15:33)*, however I don't see how it can be right to restrict someone – especially a spiritually weak someone – from worshipful actions. A sick person doesn't need their medicine taken away from them, they need their medicine given to them in order to get well!

Next scripture:

> *If anyone comes to you and <u>does not bring this teaching,</u>*
> *<u>never receive him into your homes or say a greeting to him.</u>*
> *For he that says a greeting to him is a sharer in his wicked*
> *works.*
> *– 2 John 11*

The Jehovah's Witnesses take this scripture out of the context of the times it was written: Remember, this was the newly born Christian congregation – all worship activities took place in the members' homes because there were no such things as church buildings yet. Therefore the context is that of house congregations who welcomed believers in their homes for their worship meetings. This scripture is merely stating that those house congregations were not to accept religious teachers who peddled *other* doctrine in the worship services. Instead of keeping the situation in context, though, the Jehovah's Witnesses literally take this to mean that a member must totally shun another member who doesn't happen to agree with points of doctrine.

Next scripture:

> *Moreover, if your brother commits a sin, go lay bare his*
> *fault between you and him alone. If he listens to you, you*
> *have gained your brother. But if he does not listen, take*
> *along with you one or two more, in order that at the mouth*
> *of two or three witnesses every matter may be established.*
> *If he does not listen to them, speak to the congregation. If*
> *he does not listen even to the congregation, let him be to*
> *you just as a man of the nations* **['Gentile' in some**
> **translations]** *and as a tax collector.*
> *– Matt.18:15-17*

In the Jehovah's Witness world, this means going through the proper process according to this scripture, and then completely shunning the person if they do not respond to their scriptural counsel. Unfortunately, this is another case of taking a scripture to extreme. Oh I agree that *"a man of the nations"* and *"a tax collector"* weren't highly esteemed in the early Christian congregation, however such person weren't shunned to the point of being treated as invisible or dead. In the early Christian times, such non-believers were acknowledged and shown civility and respect on a daily basis, they just weren't sought out for association and recreation. In other words, this passage is saying that the congregation should treat the erring member the same exact way you'd treat anyone else you meet that isn't a member of your faith. It isn't saying you should severely shun them.

Of course, most Jehovah's Witnesses get hung-up on the part that says *"let him be to you just as a...tax collector"*; and figure that, since tax collectors were so scorned during those times, then the ex-member should likewise be scorned; totally forgetting to get "hung-up" on how *Jesus* treated tax collectors:

> *Next, while passing along from there, <u>Jesus caught sight of a man named Matthew seated at the tax office, and he said to him: "Be my follower."</u> Thereupon he did rise up and follow him. Later, while he was reclining at the table in the house, look! many tax collectors and sinners came and began reclining with Jesus and his disciples. But on seeing this the Pharisees began to say to his disciples: "Why is it that your teacher eats with tax collectors and sinners?" Hearing [them], <u>he said: "Persons in health do not need a physician, but the ailing do. Go, then, and learn what this means, 'I want mercy, and not sacrifice.'</u> For I came to call, not righteous people, but sinners."*
> *– Matthew 9:9-13*

> *Now all the tax collectors and the sinners kept drawing near to him to hear him. Consequently both the Pharisees and the scribes kept muttering saying: "This man welcomes sinners and eats with them." Then <u>he spoke this illustration to them, saying: "What man of you with a hundred sheep, on losing one of them, will not leave the ninety-nine behind in the wilderness and go for the lost one until he finds it?</u> And when he has found it he puts it upon his shoulders and rejoices. And when he gets home he calls his friends and his neighbors together, saying to them, 'Rejoice with me, because I have found my sheep that was lost.' <u>I tell you that thus there will be more joy in heaven over one sinner that repents than over ninety-nine righteous ones who have no need of repentance</u>.*
> *– Luke 15:1-7*

The point being this: Scripture tells us to treat erring ones as tax collectors and as non-believers, (a.k.a Gentiles) (*Matthew 18:17*). Scripture also tells us to be like Jesus (*John 13:15*). Scripture also says Jesus didn't *shun* tax collectors; instead he drew them in to save them, as shown in the above passages. Therefore, to treat erring ones like a tax collector and a Gentile would mean to not associate with such ones, yet still show civility and respect in the context of bringing them back to Christianity. Note, also, that Jesus stated that the lost sheep didn't go out to find the shepherd – it was the *shepherd* who went out to find the lost sheep.

Next scripture:

> *But now I am writing you to quit mixing in company with anyone called a brother that is a fornicator or a greedy person or an idolater or a reviler or a drunkard or an extortioner, not even eating with such a man.*
> – *1.Cor. 5:11*

Again, YES, stop the association; but it doesn't say to ignore the person and act like they don't exist or that they're dead (which is how the Jehovah's Witnesses take it). Again it's another instruction to restrict association and recreation, but no instruction to be scornful, hateful, or cold-shouldered. In other words, one should acknowledge the person, yet don't accept the sin in the process.

Another point I'd like to bring out in this verse: Note that is says "quit mixing in company with anyone called a brother..." Now, in the Jehovah's Witness world, a disfellowshipped person is no longer considered to be a Jehovah's Witness. Thus, the person is no longer called "a brother". Therefore, if the person isn't called "a brother" anymore, then it would seem that he would no longer fit the parameters laid out in the scripture. I'm not saying you should freely associate with people who are willfully committing big sins; what I am saying is that such a person should have the benefit of being allowed group association with spiritually strong members as a way of encouraging the person to cease the sin.

And as a last point, I absolutely must reveal a little known piece of information that I didn't discover until just recently: In the Jehovah's Witness world, it is a well know fact that, if any member in good standing associates with a disfellowshipped member on a regular basis, then that member in good standing also risks becoming disfellowshipped too. **HOWEVER**, In the Elder's handbook **"Pay Attention To Yourselves and to All the Flock"**, in the 1991 edition, this little blurb at the bottom of page 103, last paragraph of that page :

> *"Normally, a close relative would not be disfellowshipped for associating with a disfellowshipped person unless there is spiritual association or an effort made to excuse the wrongful course."*

Therefore, during my first disfellowshipping, my family should have been able to associate with me so long as we didn't have spiritual discussions or *"excuse the wrongful course"* that I had taken. It would not have been a disfellowshipping offense for them to have a cup of coffee with me, or go to the library together, or even shop at the mall. I should have been able to enjoy secular contact with my family on a regular basis without my family fearing congregational discipline, it was right there in their own book!

However, since *only* the Elders have copies of this particular book, the rest of the congregational members had no clue that this was in there!

How convenient.

Appendix 4: Falsification of Watchtower History

One thing I didn't know until *after* I left the Jehovah's Witnesses was how they've falsified their own history over the years. Check this out:

They once believed that Christ returned in 1874:

> The Watchtower, March 1, **1923**, p. 67
> *"This proof shows that the Lord has been present since 1874"*

> The Watchtower, January 1, **1924**, p. 5
> *"Surely there is not the slightest room for doubt in the mind of a truly consecrated child of God that the Lord Jesus is present and has been since 1874"*

> Prophecy, **1929**, *p. 65, 66*
> *"The Scriptural proof is that the second presence of the Lord Jesus Christ began in 1874 AD. This proof is specifically set out in the booklet entitled Our Lord's Return."*

It was also once taught that the "time of trouble" would end in 1914.

> Zion's Watchtower, July 15 **1894**, p. 226
> *"But bear in mind that the end of 1914 is not the date for the beginning, but for the end of the time of trouble"*

> The Time Is at Hand (SS-2), 1907, p. 101
> *"The 'battle of the great day of God Almighty' (Rev. 16:14), which will end in A.D. 1914 with the complete overthrow of earth's present rulership, is already commenced."*

And then, when the end didn't happen, they had the audacity to tell the membership this:

The Watchtower Reprints, November 1, **1914**, p.5565
*Studying God's Word, we have measured the 2520 years,
the seven symbolic times, from that year 606 B.C. and have
found that it reached down to October, 1914, as nearly as
we were able to reckon. <u>We did not say positively that this
would be the year.</u>*

***After which, they began falsely teaching the <u>exact opposite</u>
of their previous teaching, saying that the Bible Students
looked forward to 1914 as the <u>coming</u> of Christ and the
<u>beginning</u> of the times of trouble:***

The Watchtower, June 15, **1954** page 370, para. 4
*Why, then, do the nations not realize and accept the
approach of this climax of judgment? It is because they
have not heeded the world-wide advertising of Christ's
return and his second presence. <u>Since long before World
War 1 Jehovah's Witnesses pointed to 1914</u> as the time for
this great event to occur.*

Awake! January 22, **1973** page 8
*...<u>Jehovah's Witnesses pointed to the year 1914, decades in
advance, as marking the start</u> of "the conclusion of the
system of things".*

The Watchtower, January 15, **1993** p. 5 para.6
*The <u>Watchtower has consistently presented evidence</u> to
honest hearted students of Bible prophecy that <u>Jesus'
presence in heavenly kingdom power began in 1914.</u>*

The Watchtower. September 15, **1998,** page 15, para.1
*"...a prophecy providentially caused sincere 19th century
Bible Students to be in expectation. By linking the "seven
times" of Daniel 4:25 with the "times of the Gentiles", they
anticipated that Christ would receive Kingdom power in
1914.*

So, they went from preaching the Coming of Christ in 1874
and the end of world troubles in 1914, to preaching the
Coming of Christ and the beginning of world-wide trouble in
1914; quietly covering the change by claiming that the newer
belief had always been in place.

Wow.

This is a big deal because The Organization consistently asserts its own supposed honesty and truthfulness while disparaging Christendom for their supposed lies. It is a very suspicious thing for The Organization to be so deceptive about their history.

All I can conclude with is this:

> ***Is This Life All There Is?*** *(Watchtower Society publication) Page 46:*
>
> *"Knowing these things, what will you do? It is obvious that the true God, who is himself "the God of truth" and who hates lies, will not look with favor on persons who cling to organizations that teach falsehood. (Psalm 31:5; Proverbs 6:16-19; Revelation 21:8) And, really, would you want to be even associated with a religion that had not been honest with you?"*

Appendix 5: False Prophecy

The Watchtower Society openly claims that they are Jehovah's Channel of Communication for mankind. This is a fact; ask any baptized Jehovah's Witness if "The Organization", or "Bethel", or "The Watchtower Society" is Jehovah's channel of communication with mankind, and they will answer affirmatively. This is backed up in their literature, as shown here:

> "*Only this organization functions for Jehovah's purpose and to his praise*. To it alone God's Sacred Word, the Bible, is not a sealed book," *(The Watchtower, July 1, 1973, p. 402).*

> "We all need help to understand the Bible, and <u>we cannot find the Scriptural guidance we need outside the 'faithful and discreet slave' organization,</u>"
> *(The Watchtower, Feb. 15, 1981).*

> All who want to understand the Bible should appreciate that the "greatly diversified wisdom of God" can become <u>known only through Jehovah's channel of communication, the faithful and discreet slave,</u>" *(The Watchtower, Oct. 1, 1994, p. 8).*

> Bear in mind that <u>our heavenly Father has an appointed channel of communication, "the faithful and discreet slave".</u> That "slave" has the responsibility to determine what information is made available to the household of faith, as well as "the proper time" for it to be dispensed. This spiritual <u>food is available only through the theocratic organization.</u> [in Watchtower speak, "theocratic organization" means only the Watchtower Society] We should always look to God's appointed channel for reliable information, not to a network of Internet users. -- Matt. 24:45
> *Our Kingdom Ministry, September 2002, p.8, para.5*

Since the boys in Bethel believe they are the "faithful and discreet slave", this means they also believe that they alone are providing "spiritual nourishment at the right time" to the membership. They develop this concept to show that the Christian congregation needs **_inspired_** "instruments" to be used as apostles, prophets, teachers, evangelizers and congregational shepherds:

> _Regarding God's channel of communication, Jesus said that the "faithful and discreet slave" would provide spiritual nourishment at the right time for all his followers and that he would set this "slave" over all his belongings._ _(Matt. 24:45-47) It is also noteworthy that the Apostle Paul, at Ephesians 4:11-16, indicated that the Christian congregation needed not only such **inspired** instruments as apostles and prophets but also as evangelizers, shepherds, and teachers to help Christians to arrive at the oneness in the faith and the accurate knowledge of the Son of God, and to gain full spiritual maturity._
> **The Watchtower, December 1, 1981 p. 27, para. 5**

Since they claim the position of being Jehovah's sole channel of communication today, and the provider of spiritual food at the right time, this can _only_ mean that they believe they actually _do_ speak in the name of Jehovah – after all, that would be the primary purpose of being His channel of communication. Being His Channel of Communication, they have also laid claim to being His modern day prophet, which they referred to as "The Jeremiah Class":

> _"So does Jehovah have a prophet to help them, to warn them of dangers and to declare things to come? These questions can be answered in the affirmative. Who is this prophet?...This "prophet" was not one man, but was a body of men and women. It was the small group of footstep followers of Jesus Christ, known at that time as International Bible Students. Today they are known as Jehovah's Christian Witnesses...Of course, it is easy to say that this group acts as a 'prophet' of God. It is another thing to prove it,"_
> **(_The Watchtower,_ April 1, 1972, p. 197).**

> _"But their refuge lies in Jehovah's provision through Christ. He sends to them the modern Jeremiah Class, with_

a message that means their salvation. No, the safety of such "Jonadabs" is not to be found in broken-down Christendom, but squarely on the side of <u>Jehovah's modern day prophet.</u>
(The Watchtower, January 1, 1978, p.22, para. 18)

One thing is now certain: If <u>the "prophet class", the Jeremiah Class,</u> is facing Har-Magedon, it is also facing the fall of Babylon the Great.
(The Watchtower, October 1, 1982, p. 27, para.9)

In this 20th century, <u>Jehovah has used the Jeremiah Class, the anointed remnant,</u> to warn the nations continually of his oncoming fury at the great tribulation.
(The Watchtower March 1, 1994 p.16, para.11)

So, at the risk of being repetitive, there is it, in their own words: They believe they are Jehovah's Channel of Communication, and are Jehovah's Modern Day Prophet. *HOWEVER*....when faced with failed prophecy or the changing of doctrine, they turn around and claim that they **_aren_**'t necessarily speaking Jehovah's words, and that they **_don't_** have the gift of prophecy, and that they are actually **_fallible_**:

*True, the brothers preparing these publications are <u>not infallible. Their writings are not inspired as are those of Paul and the other Bible writers.</u> (**2 Timothy 3:16**) And so, at times, it has been necessary, as understanding became clearer, to correct views. (**Proverbs 4:18**) However, this has resulted in a continual refining of the body of Bible-based truth to which Jehovah's Witnesses subscribe. Over the years, as adjustments have been made to that body of truth, it has become ever more wonderful and applicable to our lives in these "last days."(**And then they try to differentiate their mistakes from Christendom's by saying:**) Bible commentators of Christendom are not inspired either. Despite their claims to great knowledge, they have failed to highlight even basic Bible truths-such as the coming Paradise earth, the importance of God's name, and the condition of the dead.*
The Watchtower, February 15, 1981, pp. 18-19

*"Jehovah's Witnesses, in their eagerness for Jesus' second coming, have suggested dates that turned out to be incorrect. Because of this, some have called them false prophets. <u>Never in these instances, however, did they presume to originate predictions 'in the name of Jehovah'. Never did they say 'These are the words of Jehovah'.</u> The Watchtower, the official journal of <u>Jehovah's Witnesses has said 'We have not the gift of prophecy</u> (**January 1883, p. 425**) <u>'Nor would we have our writings reverenced or regarded as infallible'</u> (**December 15, 1896, p. 306**). The Watchtower has also said that the fact that some have Jehovah's Spirit 'does not mean those now serving as Jehovah's Witnesses are inspired. <u>It does not meant that the writings in this magazine The Watchtower are inspired and infallible and without mistakes</u> (**May 15, 1947, p. 157**). <u>The Watchtower does not claim to be inspired in its utterances, nor is it dogmatic</u> (**August 15, 1950,. p. 263**). 'The brothers preparing these publications are not infallible. <u>Their writings are not inspired as are those of Paul and the other Bible writers</u>. And so at times, it has been necessary, as understanding became clearer, to correct views"* (**February 15, 1981 p. 19**)
(**Awake! March 22, 1993, p.4**)*

Yet, even though they state that they aren't actually inspired, and don't have the gift of prophecy, they continue to treat their information as though it was really were the inspired words of God, and as though they really are prophetically gifted:

Even as <u>Bible prophecy pointed forward to the Messiah, it also directs us to the close-knit body of anointed Christian Witnesses</u> that now serve as the faithful and discreet slave. It helps us to understand the Word of God. All who want to understand the Bible should appreciate that the "greatly diversified wisdom of God" can become <u>known only through Jehovah's channel of communication, the faithful and discreet slave.</u>
(**The Watchtower, October 1, 1994, p.8**)

<u>Jehovah gives us sound counsel through his Word and through his organization, using the publications provided by "the faithful and discreet slave"</u> (Matthew 24:45, 2 Timothy 3:16). How foolish to reject good advice and insist on our own way! <u>We "must be swift about hearing"</u> when

> *Jehovah, "the one teaching men knowledge", counsels us*
> *through his channel of communication* -- *James 1:19,*
> *Psalms 94:10*
> **The Watchtower, March 15, 2003, p.27**

So now we have a sort of an oxymoron organization: An *inspired*, channel of communication from God that is *uninspired* and doesn't claim to speak the "words of Jehovah", and God's modern day prophets that do not have the gift of prophecy

This oxymoron, fence-perch position is actually very useful for them. When they teach a doctrine or a prophecy, they claim it's their status as God's Channel of Communication that gives them the power to publish such things and thus the membership must obediently follow along with it. *BUT*...when a doctrine must be changed or a prophecy is proven to fail, that's when they fall onto the other side of the fence and claim to be **un**-inspired and lacking the gift of prophecy so don't you dare berate them for making a mistake. Case in point:

At one time, they taught that 1914 would be the end of the world and the beginning of God's kingdom rulership. Note how they try to deny having set a fixed year when the prophecy failed:

> *We see no reason for changing the figures — nor could we*
> *change them if we would. They are, we believe, God's*
> *dates, not ours. But bear in mind that the end of 1914 is not*
> *the date for the beginning, but for the end of the time of*
> *trouble.*
> **The Watchtower Reprints, July 15, 1894, p. 1677**
>
> *The culmination of the trouble in October, 1914, is clearly*
> *marked in the Scriptures; and we are bound therefore to*
> *expect a beginning of that severe trouble not later than*
> *1910; — with severe spasms between now and then.*
> **The Watchtower Reprints, September 15, 1901, p. 2876**
>
> *The 'battle of the great day of God Almighty' (Rev. 16:14),*
> *which will end in A.D. 1914 with the complete overthrow of*
> *earth's present rulership, is already commenced.*
> **The Time Is at Hand (Studies in the Scriptures #2) 1907,**
> **p. 101**

Note how they turn around and deny that they set an actual fixed year once the prophecy failed:

> *Studying God's Word, we have measured the 2520 years, the seven symbolic times, from that year 606 B.C. and have found that it reached down to October, 1914, as nearly as we were able to reckon. <u>We did not say positively that this would be the year.</u>*
> **The Watchtower Reprints, November 1, 1914, p.5565**

Since that prophecy failed, they had to re-tool the teaching. Therefore, they began teaching that the coming of God's Kingdom would occur before the worldwide population who lived in 1914 died out. This was published as being the actual promise of the Creator, Jehovah:

> *As indicated on page 4, "this magazine build confidence in <u>the Creator's promise of a peaceful and secure new world before the generation that saw the events of 1914 passes away".</u>*
> **Awake! November 8, 1994, p.10**

> *<u>"Jehovah's prophetic word through Jesus Christ is: 'This generation [of 1914] will by no means pass away until all things occur.</u>' (Luke 21:32) And Jehovah, who is the source of inspired and unfailing prophecy, will bring about the fulfillmet will bring about the fulfillment of his Son's words in a relatively short time.*
> **The Watchtower, May 15, 1984, p. 6-7**

However....this very doctrine has been changed *twice* since then, the most recent being in April 2010, when they published that the "generation" was actually a much longer period of time:

> *...evidently meant that <u>the lives of the anointed who were on hand when the sign began to become evident in 1914 would overlap with the lives of other anointed ones who would see the start of the great tribulation.</u>*
> **Watchtower (Study Edition), April 15, 2010 "Holy Spirit's Role in the Outworking of Jehovah's Purpose", para. 13-14**

And thus their fence-perch works: They start off touting the prophecy of "the Creator's promise" -- meaning it would have to be Jehovah's words-- and thus the membership must abide by it. Then later they make a major change in this "Creator's promise", and make use of the "we're not inspired! We're not propheticaly gifted!" excuse as shelter against those who begin to wonder about this change.

And their sheep blindly follow whatever their told, even though their "Creator's promise" ended up being a false prophecy.

This wasn't the only time they prophesied fixed dates that didn't come true. They also prophesied that God would destroy all churches (since only the Watchtower had true Christianity) in the year 1918:

> Also, in the year 1918, when God destroys the churches wholesale and the church members by millions, it shall be that any that escape shall come to the works of Pastor Russell to learn the meaning of the downfall of 'Christianity.'
> **The Finished Mystery (Studies in the Scriptures #7) 1917 ed., p. 485**

> The parallel, therefore, would establish definitely that the harvest would close forty years thereafter; to wit, in the spring of A.D. 1918. If this be true, and the evidence is very conclusive that it is true, then we have only a few months in which to labor before the great night settles down when no man can work.
> **The Watchtower Reprints, October 1, 1917, p.6149**

> The What will the year of 1918 bring forth? This question is upon the lips of every class of men. The world looks and hopes for those things which constitute its highest ideals-- peace, plenty, health and happiness. The Christian looks for the year to bring the full consummation of the church's hopes.
> **The Watchtower Reprints, January 1, 1918, p.6191**

Obviously, this grandly anticipated event never came to pass. And this *still* wasn't the last time they tried to fix a prophetic date, as you can see:

> *"Therefore we may confidently expect that 1925 will mark the return of Abraham, Isaac, Jacob and the faithful prophets of old, particularly those named by the Apostle in Hebrews 11, to the condition of human perfection."*
> ***Millions Now Living Will Never Die, p 89 (1918)***

> *"As we have heretofore stated, the great jubilee cycle is due to begin in 1925. At that time the earthly phase of the kingdom shall be recognized .... Therefore we may confidently expect that 1925 will mark the return of Abraham...."*
> ***Millions Now Living Will Never Die, 1920, p 89***

> *"Our thought is, that 1925 is definitely settled by the Scriptures. As to Noah, the Christian now has much more upon which to base his faith than Noah had upon which to base his faith in a coming deluge."*
> ***The Watchtower, 4/1/23, p 106***

And again, they tried to disclaim their prophecy:

> *"Some anticipated that the work would end in 1925, but the Lord did not state so. The difficulty was that the friends inflated their imaginations beyond reason; and that when their imaginations burst asunder, they were inclined to throw away everything."* ***The Watchtower, p 232, 1926***

Does this mean that the Watchtower Society is a false prophet? The only way to answer this is to go by the Bible's own definition of a false prophet:

> *"However, the prophet that presumes to speak in my name a word that I have not commanded him to speak or who speaks in the name of other gods, that prophet must die. And in case you should say in your heart: "How shall we know the word that Jehovah has not spoken?" when the prophet speaks in the name of Jehovah and the word does not occur or come true, that is the word of Jehovah did not speak. With presumptuousness the prophet spoke it. You must not get frightened at him.*
> ***(Deuteronomy 18:20-22)***

This scripture leaves no wiggle room: If you make a prophecy that doesn't actually come true, then you are a false prophet, plain and simple. Just look in the Bible: Every single one of God's *true* prophets always spoke prophecy in *complete* accuracy, there was no failure and no re-tooling of the prophecy later. And, apparently, the Watchtower Society agrees with this concept, for they themselves have written:

> "True, there have been <u>those in times past who predicted an 'end to the world'</u>, even announcing a specific date. Yet nothing happened. The 'end' did not come. <u>They were guilty of false prophesying</u>. Why? What was missing?... Missing from such people were God's truths and evidence that he was using and guiding them,"
> **(Awake! Oct. 8, 1968).**

Amusingly, they don't see that their own words condemn them, since the Watchtower Society itself was apparently also missing "God's truths" when printing their erroneous teachings.

It all boils down to this: Although the Watchtower Society admits to being uninspired and lacking the gift of prophecy, their publications are expected to be treated as if they they were inspired and prophetically gifted anyway. And since they claim to be God's modern day prophet, and also claim to have no gift of prophecy, they are essentially admitting point blank that they are false prophets.

Appendix 6: Measuring Lines

For it is command upon command, command upon command, measuring line upon measuring line, measuring line upon measuring line, here a little, there a little.
– Isaiah 28:10

The Jehovah's Witnesses try to be "no part of this world" (*John 17:16*) and seek to separate themselves from the "unclean thing" (*2 Corinthians 6:14-18*). Unfortunately, in their quest for this separation from the world they make so many inane rules that they actually end up being very contradictory in their interpretations. Let's take a look at some ways in which they contradict themselves:

Thanksgiving Holiday:

In the United States, The Organization instructs the brotherhood to refrain from celebrating the Thanksgiving holiday. They wrote an extensive article in the November 22, 1976 *Awake!* magazine, covering pages 9-13. In this article they claim many different reasons why the holiday should not be celebrated. Among them: Commercialism, gluttony, promotion of alcohol, the fact that only one celebration is biblically commanded at *Luke 22:19-20*, and the fact that Christians are admonished to give thanks at all times (*Ephesians 5:20*) – not just on one special day of the year.

What is contradictory, though, is the fact that The Organization will forbid Thanksgiving, yet allow the celebration of wedding anniversaries. Why is this so inconsistent? When you think about it, the "traits" between Thanksgiving Day and a wedding anniversary are quite the same, as each celebration features the same things:

Commercialism: Thanksgiving Holiday decorations compared with anniversary gifts and jewelry, *Gluttony:* A huge turkey feast compared to a lavish anniversary feast, and *Alcohol:* Beer for the Thanksgiving football game compared with the wine or champagne as the beverage of choice for anniversaries. They also share the trait of being not commanded in scripture, as well as the trait of being a special day set aside during the year. (*Proverbs 5:18-19, Ephesians 5:20*).

Therefore, if Thanksgiving is to be shunned for the above-mentioned particular reasons, then you would think that they would also forbid the practice of celebrating one's wedding anniversary on the same grounds. But they don't, and there is no reasonable explanation for this. In essence, their dogma of avoiding Thanksgiving is nothing more than another attempt to be piously different from everyone else and nothing more.

Birthdays:

Jehovah's Witnesses do not celebrate birthdays. According to *The Watchtower* Magazine of September 1, 1992, p. 30, although birthday celebrations are rooted in superstition and false religion, these aren't *"the sole or primary reason why Jehovah's Witnesses avoid the practice"*. Eventually, though, they do come around to the main reason they forbid birthday parties: The only two birthday celebrations mentioned in scripture each involved pagans and death by decapitation (*Genesis 40:1-22, Matthew 14:6-11*). In the final paragraph, they conclude:

> *"Given the known origin of celebrating birthdays, and more important, the unfavorable light in which they are presented in the Bible, Jehovah's Witnesses have ample reason to abstain from the practice."*

They reason that, since the Bible paints birthday celebrations in such a bad light, and everything in the Bible is put there for a reason, it must mean that Christians should not be celebrating birthdays.

The contradiction lies here: Although they forbid birthday celebrations on certain grounds, they *do not* forbid wedding feasts even though such feasts also cover the same grounds as birthdays. Think about it: In scripture, just as you will not find specific references to a true believer having a celebration for his own birthday, you will likewise *not* find any specific mention of a true believer having a wedding feast for his own marriage. Although you will find a case which mentions believers being *invited* to someone's feast (***Luke 14:8***), there is no mention that these were believers' weddings. On top of that, in the one case where an actual wedding feast is described in action, one in which Jesus Christ himself attended, it is described as including a large amount of wine – a drunken party! (***John 2:2-10***). Since the only wedding feast mentioned in scripture was not mentioned as a believer's feast, and was associated with drunkenness, and since The Organization decides that everything it put into the Bible for a reason, they should be rejecting the idea of wedding feasts on the same grounds that they reject birthday celebrations.

Of course, some Jehovah's Witnesses will say that their wedding feasts are "different", because *they* don't get drunk at their weddings. My simple response is: Well, I'm sure they won't cut people's heads off at a birthday party either, so where is the difference really? Other Jehovah's Witnesses will say "God instituted marriage". My response: God also instituted the birth of Children too (***Genesis 4:1***). Again, where is the difference?

Another thing that is so contradictory is that, although birthday parties are forbidden, throwing *Baby Showers* are not. Baby Showers typically include plenty of guests, party decorations, games, cake, punch, refreshments, and loads of gifts for the baby. A baby shower exists for the sole purpose of celebrating the baby's birth – making it a *birthday party*!

Forbidding birthday parties while allowing baby showers is like forbidding you to eat lettuce but allowing you to eat a tossed salad – it's contradictory.

Beards:

Although The Organization admits that Jesus wore a beard, and that males living in the New Order will be allowed to wear beards, they still require their male membership to be clean-shaven at this time (***The Watchtower,*** May 1, 1968, p.288). Although this admonition is several decades old, to this day you will not see an active male member sport a beard or goatee. This is a classic example of them putting command upon command in the membership. The inconsistency is so blatant: Yes, Jesus wore a beard, yes, men in the New Order can have beards, no, you cannot have a beard today.

The worst part is, they don't even base this on scripture, it's all based purely on outer appearances! The above cited Watchtower articles goes on to state that Christians should be concerned with neatness, and not to be confused with the rebels in society. It states, in part (keeping in mind that all members are viewed as *ministers*):

> *"God's ministers want to avoid making any impression that would take attention away from their ministry or hinder anyone from listening to the truth. They know that people are watching true Christians very critically and that to a great extent they judge the entire congregation and the good news by the minister's appearance as a representative of the congregation".*

Basically, although there is no biblical precedent for shaving one's beard, The Organization is more concerned about outward appearances instead of focusing on the Word of God. Nevermind the fact that a man can sport a neatly trimmed beard and *still* look dignified! Nevermind the fact that many well-respected men in history wore beards: Abraham Lincoln, Frederick Douglass, Andre Tchaikovsky, etc. And of course, we cannot forget that their supposed founder, Charles Taze Russell also sported a full beard! In spite of all this though, The Organization remains rather strict about their beard policy, as I had seen when I was one of them. No baptized brother in the congregation wore a beard, not even a a well trimmed goatee. To grow anything more than a moustache was viewed as a sign of resisting the unity of the brotherhood.

Hair:

As for hair length, they require that a man's hair not grow long enough to touch the collar of his shirt. This is primarily due to the scripture at *1 Corinthians 11:14*, which says:

> *Does not nature itself teach you that if a man has long hair it is a dishonor to him*

Therefore, they do not accept long hair on males. *HOWEVER*...when it comes to the females, they totally ignore the remainder of this Bible passage which states:

> *For if a woman doesn't cover herself, let her also be shorn, but if it is disgraceful for a woman to be shorn or shaved, let her be covered...But if a woman has long hair it is a glory to her because her hair is given her instead of a headdress. However, if any man seems to dispute for some other custom, we have no other, neither do the congregations of God. (1 Corinthians 11:6, 15-16).*

In other words, they use scriptural precedent to keep the hair of male members short, and in contradiction they ignore the same scriptural precedent in order to allow the women to cut their hair. It doesn't make any sense.

As you can see from these scant few examples, they draw strict rules that end up being inconsistent and contrary to themselves.

Appendix 7: Watchtower Misquotes

The Watchtower Society is fairly infamous for misquoting its sources by dishonestly manipulating a valid quote in order to make the source sound like it supports The Society's position, when it really doesn't. Their favorite way to do this is by using ellipses ("...") to skip over the pieces of quotes that don't cater to their needs. This is something I didn't discover for myself until *after* I began trying to validate things the Watchtower Society published during my last months under them. In this section I am going to show a few of the Watchtower's quotes side by side with the *real* quotes that their misquote was taken from. I have underlined the pieces that the Watchtower Society used, so you can compare them with the parts they *did not* use:

In this first example the Watchtower publication attempts to use quotes in order to support their unitarian doctrine, even though the *real* quotes actually support a trinitarian doctrine:

> ### Watchtower Version:
> *("Should You Believe In The Trinity, p. 4)*
> *This confusion is widespread. The Encyclopedia Americana notes that the doctrine of the Trinity is considered to be "beyond the grasp of human reason."*
>
> ### The Real Quote:
> *(The Encyclopedia Americana, p. 116)*
>
> *It is held that although the doctrine is <u>beyond the grasp of human reason</u>, it is, like many of the formulations of physical science, not contrary to reason, and may be apprehended (though it may not be comprehended) by the human mind.*

Watchtower Version:
("Should You Believe in the Trinity?" p.4)
"Precisely what the doctrine is, or precisely how it is to be explained, Trinitarians are not agreed among themselves."

The Real Quote:
(A Dictionary of Religious Knowledge", Lyman Abbott, 1875, p. 944)

"It is certain, however, that from the apostolic times they paid worship to Father, Son, and Holy Ghost, addressed to them their prayers, and included them in their doxologies." ... "Precisely what the doctrine is, or precisely how it is to be explained, Trinitarians are not agreed among themselves." ... *"It is not possible for the human intellect to comprehend fully the divine nature. The Bible represents God to us as Father, Son, and Holy Ghost. It represents them as equally entitled to our highest reverence, affection, and allegiance."*

The Watchtower Society also publishes the teaching that Jesus Christ died on a singular, upright pole, a "torture stake", not a two-beamed cross. Although I do happen to agree with them on this matter, (solely due to scientific experiments performed by Dr. Frederick T. Zugibe, and Dr. Hermann Moedder) it is sad that they resorted to misquoting a source in an attempt to support their doctrine:

Watchtower Version
(Reasoning From the Scriptures, p. 89)
"The Greek word rendered "cross" in many modern Bible versions ("torture stake" in NW) is stau·ros´. In classical Greek, this word meant merely an upright stake, or pale. Later it also came to be used for an execution stake having a crosspiece. The Imperial Bible-Dictionary acknowledges this, saying: "The Greek word for cross, [stau·ros´], properly signified a stake, an upright pole, or piece of paling, on which anything might be hung, or which might be used in impaling [fencing in] a piece of ground. . . . Even amongst the Romans the crux (from which our cross is derived) appears to have been originally an upright pole."-Edited by P. Fairbairn (London, 1874), Vol. I, p. 376." Reasoning from the Scriptures p.89

The Real Quote:
"The Greek word for cross, (stauros), properly signified a stake, an upright pole, or piece of paling, on which anything might be hung, or which might be used in impaling (fencing in) a piece of ground. But a modification was introduced as the dominion and usages of Rome extended themselves through Greek-speaking countries. Even amongst the Romans, the crux (from which the word cross is derived) appears to have been originally an upright pole, and always remained the more prominent part. But from the time that it began to be used as an instrument of punishment, a traverse piece of wood was commonly added.

They would have had a much more solid argument by using real quotes from Drs. Zugibe and Moedder instead of resorting to cleverly cut-up snippets of quotes in this matter.

Oh, but this gets better. This next quote reveals a *huge* travesty in quotation, as they immediately begin the quote with dishonestly inserting the word *"Apostate"* – a word that is ***NOT*** in the original quote – in order to make the quote sound as though it is speaking only about *false* Christianity. Next, they continued the ruse by cutting out vast quantities of the *real* quote in order to keep up the facade. As you will see though, the *real* quote is speaking in regard to *all of* Christianity, not just apostasy! (I apologize in advance for the lengthiness of the real quote, but it is necessary to do so in order to show the Watchtower's deception):

Watchtower Version:
(Watchtower, April 15, 2001, p.17)
Writes historian Paul Johnson: "[Apostate] Christianity began in confusion, controversy and schism, and so it continued...The central and eastern Mediterranean in the first and second centuries AD swarmed with an infinite multitude of religious ideas, struggling to propagate themselves...From the start, then there were numerous varieties of Christianity which had little in common.

The Real Quote:

(A History of Christianity, written by Paul Johnson, Second Printing, pp.43-45)

<u>*Christianity began in confusion, controversy and schism and so it continued.*</u> *A dominant orthodox Church, with a recognizable ecclesiastical structure, emerged only very gradually and represented a process of natural selection – a spiritual survival of the fittest. And, as with such struggles, it was not particularly edifying. The Darwinian image is appropriate:* <u>*The central and eastern Mediterranean in the first and second centuries AD swarmed with an infinite multitude of religious ideas, struggling to propagate themselves.*</u> *Every religious movement was unstable and fissiparous; and these cults were not only splitting up and modulating, but reassembling in new forms. A cult had to struggle not only to survive but to retain its identity. Jesus had produced certain insights and matrices which were rapidly propagated over a large geographical area. The followers of Jesus were divided right from the start on elements of faith and practice. And the further the missionaries moved from the base, the more likely it was that their teachings would diverge. Controlling them implied an ecclesiastical organization. In Jerusalem there were "leaders" and "pillars", vaguely defined officials modelled on Jewish practice. But they were ineffective. The Jerusalem council was a failure. It outlined a consensus but could not make it work in practice. Paul could not be controlled. Nor, presumably, could others. Nor could the "pillars" of the centre party maintain their authority even in Jerusalem. They slipped back into Judaism. Then came the catastrophe of 66 – 70, and the central organization of the Church, such as it was, disappeared. It is true that the Christians now had a homogenous and extremely virile body of doctrine: the Pauline gospel, or kerygma. It stood a good chance of surviving and spreading. But it had no organization behind it. Paul did not believe in such a thing. He believed in the Spirit, working through him and others. Why should man regulate when the Spirit would do it for him? And of course he did not want a fixed system with rules and prohibitions: "If you are led by the Spirit you are not under law". The Church was an inversion of normal society. Its leaders exercised its authority through gifts of the Spirit, not*

through office. The two noblest gifts were prophecy and teaching. The apostles set the process in motion, then the Spirit took over and worked through many people: "And God has appointed in the Church first apostles, then prophets, third teachers, then workers of miracles, then healers, helpers, administrators, speakers in various kinds of tongues." Worship was still completely unorganized and subject to no special control. There was no specific organization to handle funds. And there was no distinction between a clerical class and laity. There were, indeed, presbyters in the Judaic Christian Church, but not in Paul's new convert congregations. The atmosphere in short was that of a loosely organized revivalist movement. Many, from time to time, "spoke with tongues"; all expected the parousia soon. Clerical control seemed needless and in appropriate. And the atmosphere in the Pauline churches was reproduced elsewhere, in a rapidly spreading movement. Granted this, it was inevitable that the Church expanded not as a uniform movement but as a collection of heterodoxies. Or perhaps "heterodoxies" is the wrong word, since it implies there was an orthodox version. The Pauline system did, indeed, become orthodox in time, but the other Christian versions which spread from Jerusalem were not deviations from it but evolved independently. From the start, then, there were numerous varieties of Christianity which had little in common, though they centred round belief in the resurrection.

And, incredulously, they don't stop at this type of blatantly dishonest manipulation. Another technique they have used is to *indirectly quote themselves* in order to make a point seem valid. Here's one of their examples:

Watchtower Version:

(Watchtower, May 15, 1983, p.6)
In the Italian journal Il Piccolo, of October 8, 1978, Geo Malagoli observed: "Our generation lives in a dangerous period of high seismic activity, as statistics show. In fact, during a period of 1,059 years (from 856 to 1914) reliable sources list only 24 major earthquakes causing 1,973,000 deaths. However, [in] recent disasters, we find that 1,600,000 persons have died in only 63 years, as a result of 43 earthquakes which occurred from 1915 to 1978. This

dramatic increase further goes to emphasize another accepted fact-our generation is an unfortunate one in many ways."

They say they are quoting the Italian magazine "Il Piccolo", which is technically true. However, what is "Il Piccolo" quoting? Nothing other than a previous *Awake* magazine! Check it out:

Awake!, February 22, 1977, p. 11
Interestingly, for a period of 1,059 years (856 – 1914 CE), reliable sources list only 24 major earthquakes, with 1,972,952 fatalities. But compare that with the accompanying partial list citing 43 instances of earthquakes, in which 1,579,209 persons died during just the 62 years from 1915 to 1976 CE.

In short, the May 15, 1983 Watchtower is quoting the October 1978 Il Piccolo, which is actually, itself, quoting the February 1977 Awake.

Ingenious!

It keeps going. On occasion, they've also manipulated quotes that are actually pro-trinitarian to make it *sound* like they support the Jehovah's Witness anti-trinitarian doctrine:

Watchtower Version:
(Should You Believe in the Trinity?, p.11)
"The trinity was a major preoccupation of Egyptian theologians . . . Three gods are combined and treated as a single being, addressed in the singular. In this way the spiritual force of Egyptian religion shows a direct link with Christian theology." Thus, in Alexandria, Egypt, churchmen of the late third and early fourth centuries, such as Athanasius, reflected this influence as they formulated ideas that led to the Trinity. Their own influence spread, so that Morenz considers "Alexandrian theology as the intermediary between the Egyptian religious heritage and Christianity."

The Real Quote:
(Egyptian Religion, Siegfried Morenz, pp. 254-257)

> *The trinity was a major preoccupation of Egyptian*
> *theologians. ... three gods are combined and treated as a*
> *single being, addressed in the singular. In this way the*
> *spiritual force of Egyptian religion shows a direct link with*
> *Christian theology. In order to avoid any gross*
> *misunderstanding, we must at once emphasize that the*
> *substance of the Christian Trinity is of course Biblical:*
> *Father, Son and Holy Ghost. The three are mentioned*
> *alongside one another in the New Testament, probably for*
> *liturgical reasons.*
>
> *Without abandoning our principle that Egyptian influence*
> *made itself felt as an undercurrent throughout Hellenism,*
> *we may nevertheless claim pride of place for Alexandria*
> *and so consider <u>Alexandrian theology as the intermediary*
> *between the Egyptian religious heritage and Christianity.</u>*
> *The Trinity is not the only subject- matter at issue here.*
> *Also Christology, which is closely linked to it - the doctrine*
> *concerning the nature of Christ and especially his pre-*
> *existence before the creation and time - revolves around*
> *questions which had been posed earlier by Egyptian*
> *theologians and which they solved in a strikingly similar*
> *way.*

And then, I found something else that was interesting. In the May 15, 1977 *TheWatchtower*, pp. 319 – 320 ("Questions From Readers"), the Watchtower Society quoted Bible translator William Barclay in a way that sounded as though he agreed with The Watchtower Society's published view that **John 1:1** does not support the Trinity. This is their version of William Barclay's quote:

Watchtower Version:
What is interesting is that in John 1:1 the definite article o [ho] is not used in front of theos when applied to the Son, the Word. Regarding this point the noted Bible translator William Barclay writes:

"Now, normally, except for special reasons, Greek nouns always have the definite article in front of them...When a Greek noun has not got the article in front of it, it becomes rather a description than an identification, and has the character of an adjective rather than of a noun. We can see exactly the same in English. If I say: "James is the man", then I identify James with some definite man whom I have

in mind; but if I say "James is man" then I am simply describing James as human, and the word man has become a description and not an identification. If John had said ho theos en ho logos, using a definite article in front of both nouns, then he would have definitely identified the logos [the Word] with God, but because he has no definite article in front of theos, it becomes a description, and more of an adjective than a noun. The translation then becomes, to put it rather clumsily, "The Word was in the same class as God, belonged to the same order of being as God"...John is not here identifying the Word with God. To put it very simply, he does not say that Jesus was God.
(Many Witnesses, One Lord (1963), pages 23, 24

HOWEVER...the *real* Barclay quote in its entirety actually says all *this*:

The Real Quote:

"In a matter like this, we cannot do other than to go to the Greek, which is theos en ho logos. Theos is the Greek word for God, en for was, ho for the, logos for word. Now normally, except for special reasons, Greek nouns always have the definite article in front of them, and we can see at once here that theos the noun for God has not got the definite article in front of it. When a Greek noun has not got the article in front of it, it becomes rather a description than an identification, and has the character of an adjective than of a noun. We can see exactly the same in English. If I say, "James is the man," then I identify James with some definite man whom I have in mind; but if I say: "James is man", then I am simply describing James as human, and the word man has become a description and not an identification. If John had said ho theos en ho logos, using a definite article in front of both nouns, then he would have definitely identified the Logos with God, but because he has no definite article in front of theos it becomes a description, and more of an adjective than a noun. The translation then becomes, to put it rather clumsily, "The Word was in the same class as God, belonging to the same order of being as God." The only modern translator who fairly and squarely faced this problem is Kenneth Wuest, who has: "The Word was as to his essence essential deity." But it is here that the NEB has brilliantly solved the problem with the absolutely accurate

> *rendering: "What God was the Word was." <u>John is not here</u>*
> <u>*identifying the Word with God. To put it very simply, he*</u>
> <u>*does not say that Jesus was God"*</u> *(William Barclay; Many*
> *Witnesses, One Lord, p23-24)*
>
> *"God himself took this human flesh upon him." (William*
> *Barclay; Many Witnesses, One Lord, p27)*

William Barclay got news of this terrible misquote when Donald Shoemaker, a professor from Biola College (now named Biola University), wrote to Barclay regarding this Watchtower misquote. Barclay responded to him in a letter dated August 26th, 1977, in this way:

> *Dear Professor Donald Shoemaker,*
>
> *Thank you for your letter of August 11th. The Watchtower article has, by judicious cutting, made me say the opposite of what I meant to say. What I was meaning to say, as you well know, is that Jesus is not the same as God, to put it more crudely, that he is of the same stuff as God, that is of the same being as God, but the way the Watchtower has printed my stuff has simply left the conclusion that Jesus is not God in a way that suits themselves. If they missed from their answer the translation of Kenneth Wuest and the N.E.B., they missed the whole point. It was good of you to write and I don't think I need say anything more to make my position clear.*
>
> *With every good wish.*
>
> *Yours Sincerely*
>
> *William Barclay.*

It is also interesting to note that this *isn't* the first time that Barclay outed the dishonest twistings of truth by the Watchtower Society. In the *Expository Times*, dated November of 1953, he previously spoke regarding the Watchtower Society's rendering of the New Testament in their *"New World Translation of the Holy Scriptures"* Bible, saying:

> *The deliberate distortion of the truth by this sect is seen in their New Testament translation which is grammatically impossible. It is abundantly clear that a sect which can translate the New Testament like that is intellectually dishonest.*

Of course, these aren't the only misquoted items the Watchtower Society has published. *Every single year* you can find where they've misquoted something in their literature in ways that are skewed to their doctrine – it would take several volumes of books to reveal them all! When I was first informed of their penchant for misquoting sources, I was quite skeptical at first, even though I no longer believed in their denomination. I naively believed that they would be too smart to resort to that kind of dishonesty – it's too easy to check the sources and reveal the fraud! But once I was challenged to actually check the sources, I found how true this accusation was.

Again, I was hit in the head with it: Never take a religious leader's words at face value; always *always* check the facts thoroughly first.

Appendix 8: New Light

Jehovah's Witnesses look at themselves as progressive. They are taught that their knowledge will change over time as God progressively gives them a better understanding of truth. They call this progression "new light". When "new light" is given, it is given with the implication that the membership should be thrilled with the updated understanding. The idea is that the progression of "new light" indicates being another step closer to The End, which is when Armageddon happens and the New Order begins. This idea of "new light" is taken from ***Proverbs 4:18***, which says:

> *"But the path of the righteous ones is like the bright light that is getting lighter and lighter until the day is firmly established".*

The Organization claims to be God's appointed channel of communication, and that only *they* can provide "accurate knowledge" to mankind. Since Jehovah is a God of truth (***Psalms 31:5***), and cannot lie (***Hebrews 6:18***), then the information they provide would *have to be* true and accurate. However, if this were fact, then why is there a need for them to continually *correct* this so-called accurate information with "new light"? They explain it by claiming that it's a matter of the light getting brighter, as mentioned in the verse quoted above; brighter "light", a.k.a clearer understanding, would require a tweaking of doctrine to reflect that clarified understanding. Simple enough, right?

The unspoken problem with "new light", though is that, at times, it *totally* contradicts a previous teaching. Of course, they have this problem covered, as explained here:

> *However, it may have seemed to some as though that path has not always gone straight forward. At times explanations given by Jehovah's visible organization have shown adjustments, seemingly to previous points of view. But this has not actually been the case. This might be*

> *compared to what is known in navigational circles as*
> *"tacking". By maneuvering the sails the sailors can cause*
> *a ship to go from right to left, back and forth, but all the*
> *time making progress towards the destination in spite of*
> *contrary winds."*
> **The Watchtower, December 1, 1981 p. 27, para. 2**

Especially notice the part that said

> *"... At times explanations given by Jehovah's visible*
> *organization have shown adjustments, seemingly to*
> *previous points of view. But this has not actually been the*
> *case..."*

Here's the kicker: They absolutely *have* returned to "previous points of view" in spite of this denial! Their problem is, since they claim to be the channel of God, and supposedly God made a change that was a progression forward, then a change that goes *backwards* works against the ideals of their indoctrination. Although they deny returning to previous points of view, the fact is that they *have* done such a thing. One notorious example of this return to previous points of view can be seen here:

> **Will the people killed by God in Sodom and**
> **Gomorrah be resurrected in the New Order?**
> *NO* – *The Watchtower, June 1, 1952 page 338*
> *YES* –*The Watchtower , July 15, 1979 page 8*
> *NO* – *The Watchtower, June July 1, 1988 page 31*
> *YES* – *Insight on the Scriptures, Volume 2 p.985 (1988)*
> *YES and NO? – Early printings of the book "You Can Live*
> *Forever on a Paradise Earth" say "yes", but later*
> *printings of the same book say "no" (pages 178-179), a*
> *fact pointed out in the Watchtower's Our Kingdom Ministry*
> *sheet dated December 1989, on page 7*

Another notorious example:

Is the medical use of blood fractions scriptural?

NO – *Awake! Sept. 8, 1956 Awake, p. 20*
YES-- The Watchtower Sept. 15, 1958 p. 575
NO – The Watchtower Sept. 15, 1961 pp.558-559
YES-- Awake! Aug. 22, 1965 Awake, p. 18

And then there's this truly sad example:

When it comes to rape, is the woman guilty of sexual sin if she doesn't scream, even under threat of a knife or gun?

YES – *The Watchtower, June 1 1968, pp.345-350*
NO – *Awake! July 8, 1980, pp. 5-6*
YES – *Awake! February 22, 1984, p. 27, para.*
NO – *Awake! March 1993, pp. 4-5*
YES – *The Watchtower, December 1998, p. 25 footnote*

How can they seriously claim that they haven't actually returned to previous points of view when their own literature shows otherwise? These changes aren't a matter of "tacking", because the act of tacking actually takes the boat *forward*. Into Instead, this is more like a boat continually returning *backward* to it's original starting point!

But of course, this teaching about tacking also got its own "new light", though I'm not so sure they realized it when they printed this:

> *Seeing the strenuous efforts needed to succeed in the race for life, Paul went on to say: "Therefore, the way I am running is not uncertainly; the way I am directing my blows is so as not to be striking the air" (1 Corinthians 9:26). The word "uncertainly" literally means "unevidently" (Kingdom Interlinear*), "unobserved, unmarked" (Lange's Commentary). Hence, <u>to run "not uncertainly" means that to every observer it should be very evident where the runner is heading. The Anchor Bible renders it "not on a zigzag course". If you saw a set of footprints that meanders up and down the beach, circles around now and then, and even goes backwards at times, you would hardly think the person was running at all, let alone that he had any idea where he was heading. But if you saw a set of footprints that form a long, straight line,</u> each footprint ahead of the*

> *previous one and all evenly spaced, <u>you would conclude</u> <u>that the footprints belong to the one who knows exactly</u> <u>where he is going.</u>*
> (***The Watchtower, August 1, 1992 page 17, paragraph 16***)

So, of course, this begs the question: Does The Organization have a history of walking it's teachings in a straight line or not? Let's take a look at their teachings on blood and organ donation – does it walk a straight line, or a confusing one? Judge for yourself:

> **1.** Blood transfusions are viewed as an organ donation. (*How Can Blood Save Your Life? p.8, 1990*)

> **2.** And organ donations are acceptable. (The Watchtower *March 15, 1980 p.31*)

> **3.** *HOWEVER*, whole-blood transfusions are forbidden. (*How Can Blood Save Your Life? p.27, 1990*)

> **4.** And, although, they forbid the transfusion of whole- blood, they do not forbid the transfusion of the individual parts ("fractions") that make up the whole blood. (*The Watchtower, June 15, 2004 p.21 para. 10-12, & p.30*)

> **5.** The use of "fractions" is allowed because these parts naturally pass from mother to child within the womb (*The Watchtower, June 1, 1990 pages 30-31*).

> 6. Interestingly, though, they continued to forbid the transfusion of whole white blood cells, even though these also naturally pass from mother to baby in breast milk!

This hodge-podge of doctrine is *not* moving ahead in a purposeful straight line, and it's certainly not "tacking" – it's running around willy nilly! When I was a devout Jehovah's Witness I was so confused by these things that I, once again, defaulted to the "wait on Jehovah" mode.

However, once the Lord opened my eyes, I realized that I should have applied the scripture at *1 Corinthians 14:33*

"For God is not the author of confusion, but of peace, as in all churches of the saints" (KJV).

Sometimes, though, new light isn't quite as complicated as the above examples. More often it can simply be a switch from one point of view to another, without returning to previous "Light". This has happened on many occasions when it comes to interpretation of scripture, interpretation of prophecy, and cultural / legal understanding of matters. Members are told that, since all are merely human, we cannot possibly understand everything all at once. Therefore, Jehovah progressively gives us only the amount of information we can absorb at one time (This is part of the Faithful and Discreet Slave giving us the "proper food at the proper time" dogma). So *this* begs the question: Does "new light" always give a clearer understanding of previous information?

No, it does not. Case in point:

When I was young, the Watchtower Society was publishing that Christ's words *"this generation will by no means pass away until all these things occur"* at *Matthew 24:34* meant that Armageddon would come before the generation of people alive in 1914 died out:

> *The Watchtower, May 15, 1984pages 6-7 article*
> *"The Generation Will Not Pass Away"*
> *Form a purely human veiwpoint, it could appear that these developments could hardly take place before the generation of 1914 disappears from the scene. But fulfillments of all the foretold events affecting the generation of 1914 does not depend on comparatively slow human action. Jehovah's prophetic word through Christ Jesus is: "This generation [of 1914] will by no means pass away until all things occur." (Luke 21:32) And Jehovah, who is the source of inspired and unfailing prophecy, will bring about the fulfillment of his Son's words in a relatively short time.*

The Watchtower, May 1, 1985 page 4 article "Is God Delaying His Judgment?"

...Bible chronology and the fulfillment of Bible prophecy provide ample proof that this time period began in 1914. thus <u>before the 1914 generation completely dies out, God's judgment must be executed</u>...

This information was to be regarded as accurate knowledge and truth from Jehovah. *HOWEVER*, in 1995 they completely changed the *entire* meaning of "this generation" with new light:

The Watchtower, November 1, 1995 p19-20, para. 12, 15 "A Time to Keep Awake"

Therefore, in the final fulfillment of Jesus' prophecy today, <u>"this generation" apparently refers to the peoples of the earth who see the sign of Christ's presence but fail to mend their ways.</u> In contrast, we as Jesus' disciples refuse to be molded by the life-style of "this generation". Though in the world, we must be no part of it, "for the appointed time is near" (Revelation 1:3, John 17:16)...Does our <u>more precise viewpoint</u> on "this generation" mean that Armageddon is further away than we had thought? Not at all! ...

Although they claim precision in this information, this clearly isn't a matter of being "more precise", as precision would mean focusing closer to the original viewpoint; instead, this is a matter of veering to a completely *other* viewpoint! But this wasn't the end of the matter, as the April 15, 2010 Watchtower changed the meaning of "this generation" yet again!

The Watchtower, April 15, 2010 (Study Edition Article), para.13-14
"HOLY SPIRIT'S ROLE IN THE OUTWORKING OF JEHOVAH'S PURPOSE "

13 Third, holy spirit is at work in bringing Bible truths to light. (Prov. 4:18) This magazine has long been used by "the faithful and discreet slave" as the primary channel for dispensing increased light. (Matt. 24:45) For example, consider our understanding of those who make up "this generation" mentioned by Jesus. (Read Matthew 24:32-

34.) To what generation did Jesus refer? The article "Christ's Presence—What Does It Mean to You?" explained that Jesus was referring, not to the wicked, but to his disciples, who were soon to be anointed with holy spirit. Jesus' anointed followers, both in the first century and in our day, would be the ones who would not only see the sign but also discern its meaning—that Jesus "is near at the doors."

14 What does this explanation mean to us? Although we cannot measure the exact length of "this generation," we do well to keep in mind several things about the word "generation": It usually refers to people of varying ages whose lives overlap during a particular time period; it is not excessively long; and it has an end. (Ex. 1:6) How, then, are we to understand Jesus' words about "this generation"? He evidently meant that the lives of the anointed who were on hand when the sign began to become evident in 1914 would overlap with the lives of other anointed ones who would see the start of the great tribulation. That generation had a beginning, and it surely will have an end. The fulfillment of the various features of the sign clearly indicate that the tribulation must be near. By maintaining your sense of urgency and keeping on the watch, you show that you are keeping up with advancing light and following the leadings of holy spirit.—Mark 13:37.

So here we have the changes in a nutshell:

1984 Version: *"This Generation" refers to all the people in the world who were already alive during 1914.*

1995 Version: *"This Generation" refers to the world wide population who see the signs of Christ's presence but do nothing to mend their ways*

2010 Version: *"This Generation" refers to the anointed ones of Jehovah who were on hand when the sign of Christ's presence began in 1914, overlapping with the lives of later anointed ones who would see the beginning of the Great Tribulation.*

And the really sad thing is, the first meaning was to be viewed as completely accurate when it came out, then the second meaning was to be viewed as completely accurate when *it* came out, and *then* this newly updated meaning is to be viewed as completely accurate as it came out. Can anyone honestly say that these different versions are all honing in on a more *clearer* understanding of "this generation"? NO – these are all different takes on the idea, not a progression of better understanding from an original idea!

Obviously, since all of these takes are different, then they cannot all be accurate, meaning there has actually been *inaccuracy* coming from the "faithful and discreet slave". And, inaccurate information is the same exact thing as false information, something the Watchtower Society would call a lie; there is no difference. In essence, their putting forth of "new light" on this (or any other) matter basically shows them to have a tendency towards inaccurate, and false knowledge, and obviously *not* dispensing *"proper food at the proper time"* as they've been claiming.

Of course, this doesn't go unnoticed, and so the Society will periodically state from time to time that they are not inspired prophets of God and are fallible.(***Reasoning From the Scriptures*** p. 136, December 1, 2002 ***The Watchtower***, p. 17, paragraph 18). Along with this, they also state that God allows their erroneous understandings to exist in order to sift out loyal members from disloyal members (***The Watchtower,*** December 1, 1981, p. 31, par. 19, March 15 1996 ***The Watchtower,*** March 15, 1996 pp. 16-17, par. 9-10).

My response to their explanations:

Since when does the God of *truth* (***Psalms 31:5***), test His people with *false information*? God hates lies (***Proverbs 6:16-19***), because lies are evil (***John 8:44***). In scripture, a person's faith was *never* proven by obedience to lies or false teachings, instead a person's faith was always proven one's *actions*! Cases in point:

Samaritan Woman *proved her faith by bringing the town to see Christ (John 4:1-29)*
Bleeding Woman *proved her faith by touching Christ's robe (Matthew 9:20-22)*
Abraham *proved his faith by acting upon God's request for sacrifice (Genesis 22),*
Israelites *proved their faith by smearing blood on their doorposts (Exodus chapter 12)*
Paralytic *proved his faith by tearing a hole in a roof to access Jesus (Mark 2:1-12)*
Rahab *proved her faith by hiding the Israelite spies (Joshua chapter 2)*
David *proved his faith by going against a warrior with a mere slingshot (1 Samuel 17)*
Noah *proved his faith by building the ark amid criticism (Genesis Chapter 6)*
Ruth *proved her faith by abandoning her people for God's instead (Ruth Chapter 1)*

In contrast, anytime God's people followed false or inaccurate teachings, they were considered to be *unfaithful* against God. Cases in point:

Paul chastised various congregations for tolerating inaccurate teachings:
The Corinthians (2 Corinthians 11:3-4)
The Galatians (Galatians 1:6-9)
Warned some congregations to avoid inaccurate deceptions, lest the wrath of God come upon them
The Ephesians (Ephesians 5:6-11)
The Colossians (Colossians 2:8, 16-23)
To Timothy (1 Timothy 4:16, 2 Timothy 2:16-17, 2 Timothy 4:3-5)
Scripture praises the ones who didn't tolerate the inaccurate teachings:
Acts 17:10-11

Nowhere in scripture is obedience to false / inaccurate teachings a mark of Christian loyalty. In fact, I am reminded of the scripture at *2 Timothy 6:20-21*, which says:

> *O Timothy, guard what is laid up in trust with you, turning away from the empty speeches that violate what is holy and from the contradictions of the falsely called "knowledge" For making a show of such knowledge some have deviated from the faith.*

However, in the Jehovah's Witness world, if a member chooses to resist a teaching from The Organization, they are targeted as spiritually weak, possibly even an apostate. It doesn't matter if the member has solid scriptural backing for their position; In order to keep one's good standing in the congregation, one must accept the teaching, at least outwardly if nothing else. In essence, The Organization is teaching loyalty to *The Organization*, not to God.

Appendix 9: Sacrifice vs. Mercy

Jehovah's Witnesses tend to be severely legalistic when it comes to upholding their doctrine. They are much more concerned about congregational "cleanness" than plight of a member in a life-or-death situation. Although scriptures states:

> *"Go then, and learn what this means; 'I want mercy, and not sacrifice'. For I came to call, not righteous people, but sinners"* (**Matthew 9:13**)

The Jehovah's Witnesses tend to put sacrifice ahead of the mercy. Case in point:

Blood Transfusions: At the time of this writing, Jehovah's Witnesses allow the acceptance of blood *fractions*, but not the acceptance of whole blood or whole blood components. Their avoidance of whole blood is based on these two scriptures:

> *"...abstain from things polluted by idols and from fornication and from what is strangled and from blood."* (***Acts 15:20***)

> *"...they should keep themselves from what is sacrificed to idols as well as from blood and what is strangled and from fornication"* (***Acts 21:25***)

According to The Organization, The primary components of blood are considered to be: Red cells, white cells, platelets, and plasma. However, because The Organization has chosen to split hairs on the matter, they decided that blood fractions are so processed and removed from blood that they are no longer considered to be blood and is therefore a "conscience matter" for the individual member, whereas whole blood is still blood and must be forbidden. Interestingly, the Watchtower also states that:

> "...when it comes to fractions of *any* of the primary components, each Christian, after careful and prayerful meditation, must conscientiously decide for himself" (**The Watchtower, June 15, 2004 pp. 29-31**).

In other words, although one could be disfellowshipped for taking whole blood or any of the Watchtower-designated "primary components", one could *not* be disfellowshipped for taking any of the fractions of those very same primary components. Essentially, this means that a Jehovah's Witness can take every ingredient in blood, just not all at the same time. That is the same as forbidding someone to eat a salad, but allowing that someone to eat each of the salad's ingredients separately.

It's ridiculous.

Therefore, in the Jehovah's Witness world, a hemophiliac can righteously receive a transfusion of clotting factors in order to stem the bleeding from a small paper cut, but an accident victim profusely gushing blood must righteously refuse a transfusion of packed red blood cells.

What's more is the fact that Jehovah's Witnesses are not allowed to donate blood, (*Watchtower, October 15, 2000, p. 31*) even though they are allowed to take the blood fractions. This is a serious matter, since the *only* way to obtain blood fractions is through those forbidden blood donations! Realize that blood donors don't donate *fractions*, they donate *whole blood!* This is because, In order to obtain, "fractions", whole blood is needed in order to sift out those fractions! This means that Jehovah's Witnesses are taught to deplete from the blood supply without replenishing it.

It's shameful.

AUTHOR'S POST SCRIPT

Although many will believe otherwise, this book is not meant to be hateful or demeaning to the Jehovah's Witness way of life. I don't see them as my enemy, rather I see them as misled people who need to find the true light of Jesus Christ. I cannot answer for how the leaders in Bethel decide doctrine, but it is apparent that their followers are blind sheep who are unknowingly following the wrong shepherd. They do not need our derision, instead they need our prayers.

Do not use this book as a way of attacking them or being confrontational. This book is only for educational purposes, so that the reader can understand the Jehovah's Witness mindset better when trying to reach out to them.

God Bless!

Notes:

5856410R0

Made in the USA
Charleston, SC
11 August 2010